Cleveland

sHRm
Society for Human Resource Management

Janet Collins

B

HOW TO GET FROM
CUBICLE
TO
CORNER OFFICE

HOW TO GET FROM
CUBICLE
TO
CORNER OFFICE

Joel Weiss

Gibbs Smith, Publisher
Salt Lake City

First Edition
08 07 06 05 04   5 4 3 2 1

Published by
Gibbs Smith, Publisher
P.O. Box 667
Layton, UT 84041
Orders: 1.800.748.5439
www.gibbs-smith.com

Designed by Gotham Design
Printed and bound in U.S.A.

Library of Congress Cataloging-in-Publication Data
Weiss, Joel (Joel J.)
    How to get from cubicle to corner office/ Joel Weiss.—1st ed.
        p. cm.
    ISBN 1–58685–524–7
    1. Career development. 2. Vocational guidance. I. Title.
HF5381.W4343 2005
650.14–dc22

                                            2004020417

"It is one of the most beautiful compensations of life,
that no man can sincerely try to help another
without helping himself."
— Ralph Waldo Emerson

"No one is useless in the world
who lightens the burden of it for anyone else."
— Charles Dickens

"A must-read for anyone who cares about their career, *How To Get From Cubicle to Corner Office* lays out the steps to career success in a way that is easy to understand and fun to read. If you only read one business book this year, make it *How To Get From Cubicle to Corner Office!*"

— Chester Elton
Co-author of *Managing With Carrots,*
The 24 Carrot Manager and *A Carrot A Day*

"I refer to Joel Weiss' book prior to many of our company meetings and use examples to help make a point. I can't say enough about the value of this book. It is the only one of my many business books that I read over and over. It is one of those rare books that applies to both business and life."

— Dean Skinner
President Interactive Services
Bennett Adelson & Co.

"This book is a brilliant and simple primer of fundamentals for life and career. It is the essential foundation for people competing in this new world of globalization. I believe the formulas Joel Weiss presents are absolute requirements for everyone who wants to succeed. This is must reading for all people who want to make a difference and all companies who want to compete."

— Donna Rae Smith
CEO and Founder, Bright Side
Author of *The Power of Building Your Bright Side*

"Having worked almost exclusively with upper-level management, I have seen these principles applied and the success they can ensure. What is amazing about *How To Get From Cubicle to Corner Office* is that these principles are all spelled out in one reader-friendly book. Don't be fooled by its simplicity, for it holds the path to increased success."

— Judith A. Piani
CGA, President and CEO Piani & Co.
Author of *Trade Secrets*

"This is an incredible book. I've read it several times and learn more each time. An easy-read, quick-reference guide when you need a common-sense solution. A no-nonsense approach with no gimmicks, just about doing the right thing by a very insightful and professional veteran."

> — Mark Cerame
> Managing Partner
> Business Development, Arras Group

"An excellent tool for students prior to starting a career. I only wish I had had this book at the beginning of *my* career. It certainly would have made the path to success much easier."

> — Donald Salsburg
> Associate Counsel (retired)
> Prudential Financial

"This is the stuff that gets good people promoted to the corner office . . . simple techniques and insights to quickly advance your career that are never taught in college and seldom learned on the job . . . until it is too late."

> — Philip Yaeger
> Vice President
> Adcom Communications

"Weiss has created a primer for the student of business life. Whether you have been formally trained or are a graduate of Hard Knocks U., this book offers the sometimes-elusive common sense for the business place."

> — Joshua Fischer, Ph.D
> Regional Dean
> Indiana Wesleyan University

"A very well written book thorough and easy to read. Especially valuable for young people getting ready to begin a career. My three children are reading this book. I strongly recommend it.

> — Dr. Gregory Classen, D.O.
> Chief of Plastic and Reconstructive Surgery
> South Point Hospital Cleveland Clinic Health System;
> Associate Professor, Ohio University

FOREWORD   10

ACKNOWLEDGMENTS   12

INTRODUCTION   13

PART ONE: PROFESSIONAL PRACTICES
TO GET YOU NOTICED

   1. Present the Unshakable Facts   17

   2. Use Information to Reach Good Conclusions   24

   3. Tackle Problems Head-On   28

   4. Communicate Confidently   32

   5. Don't Try to Go It Alone   36

   6. Track Vital Life Signs   42

   7. Be an Eager Learner   46

   8. Ask for What You Want   49

   9. Package Yourself for Sale   51

  10. Plan Your Career   56

  11. Prepare for Meetings   61

  12. Get Involved in Company Planning   65

  13. Network with Consultants   70

  14. Sharpen Your Management Skills   74

PART TWO: PERSONAL TRAITS AND PRACTICES TO DEVELOP

15. Have a Positive Attitude   82

16. Be Responsive and Reliable   87

17. Be a Doer, Not Just a Talker   92

18. Anticipate and Adapt to Change   95

19. Be Open and Friendly   99

20. Put in Extra Time and Effort   104

21. Help People   108

22. Have a Caring Heart   112

23. Be Gracious at Winning and Losing   115

24. Learn to Enjoy Your Work   118

25. Choose the Best Role Models   122

26. Review Your Career   126

27. Strive to Be Fair   130

28. Develop Faith for the Tough Times   134

RECAP   137

SUMMARY   141

ABOUT THE AUTHOR   144

Joel Weiss and I first met in the summer of 1983 during my orientation visit to Burger King Corporation before becoming chief financial officer. I was immediately impressed with Joel's maturity, experience, and simple wisdom. Over the next five years, Joel, as an executive vice president and chief administrative officer, and I worked closely together on a number of projects at Burger King. I always knew I could count on Joel for thoughtful analyses well-prepared and on time; a steady, un-hysterical point of view; and complete honesty.

Now, for the benefit of the next generation of leaders, Joel has condensed decades of his corporate, military, and personal experiences into this easy-to-read, informative operations manual on how to survive and prosper in today's organizations. Laced with stories from his intriguing past and sprinkled with lesser-known, thought-provoking quotations from a variety of sources, Joel gently leads the reader through a series of valuable suggestions on how to improve your performance and get noticed in the process.

This helpful book reinforces the importance of having your facts straight, your career planned, and your appetite for aggressive learning undiminished. It clarifies your need for real life skills, such as having a great attitude, a good heart, and a strong faith. The book reminds you to be pleasant but not a push-over; to give credit to others but save some for yourself; and to simultaneously work hard *and* smart.

This is an ideal book and resource for a recent graduate, a new employee just embarking on a career, or for anyone who simply needs to be reminded that victory, more often than not, is the result of the persistent application of common sense.

Charles S. Olcott
Former CEO, Burger King Corporation

T here are always a few special people who should be recognized for their help and advice in getting a book written and published.

I was fortunate to have a number of people, all experts in their own fields, read and critique this book. I'd like to thank Jeff Asfour, Antony Brilakis, Mark Cerame, Dr. Greg Classen, Sharon Dietrick, Chester Elton, Ron McDougall, Charlie Olcott, Tom Rea, Al Ries, Dean Skinner, Donna Rae Smith, Jack Trout, Bernie Willett, John Wurzburger, and Phil Yaeger.

A special thanks to Christopher Robbins and the professional staff at Gibbs Smith, Publisher, for all their support and confidence in this book.

My four children, Sara, Dan, Laura, and John, all successful in their own right, took the time to read every word and constructively critique the book.

My wife Carol added her own honest and humorous opinions about everything.

This book is about achieving success and the part people play in that adventure. People have always helped me and once again they did here.

In 1989, having just taken early retirement from my position as executive vice president and chief administrative officer at Burger King Corporation, I was invited to speak to a class of seniors at Washington State University about strategy in the fast food business. In addition to describing the workings of a highly competitive segment of the restaurant industry, I took the opportunity to reflect on my career and offer some advice about entering the workforce. My comments were well received, and I started to think about compiling what I considered to be important tips and skills that could help young people to get a good, solid start in their careers. I also realized that the information could help jump-start those who felt stuck in their cubicles. Over the years this project had interruptions, but I never forgot the goal, in part because I was often reminded by so many people who ignored the fundamental building blocks for success.

My goal is not to cover all topics in great depth. Rather, this is a handbook of the basics; other books are available with more in-depth information on specific subjects that you should eventually read. This book deals with the large and small requirements for success in your job, your career, and your life.

I recognize that time is a big factor in determining what you read. Our time is precious and the demands of everyday business make it difficult to read and learn as much as we would like. You can read this book quickly and use the tools immediately to make your job easier and more enjoyable, and to achieve more on your way to the corner office. **The book is organized in two parts: the *professional* practices you need and the *personal* traits and practices that are also vital to achieving success. Each chapter has a message that can be applied right now.** It will help you to succeed because every tip and suggestion has been tried and proven to work. Combining some or all of these ideas will have a very favorable effect on your career. And all of this information can be applied to most any job in any industry.

I have had fifty years of experience in the military and business, working in diverse industries from information technology to fast food. I have worked for many different kinds of companies and lived and worked in several countries. I always looked for ways to achieve and tools that would help me stand out and not miss what was important. For the most part, I learned the fundamentals of success through observation. I had both good and bad role models, and I learned from both.

A few years ago when I started listing what I had learned over a long career, I recognized there were principles that people ignored or did not use consistently. I knew that if people did all or most of these things they would greatly enhance their chance for success. While it took me many years to make good use of these ideas, I would have done it much sooner if someone had given me this book earlier in my career. It's in this spirit that I pass on these simple tools and suggestions that should make a real difference in your career.

Donna Rae Smith, the founder and president of Bright Side, a successful company that teaches team-building and leadership skills, suggested that knowing the fundamentals described here would position the reader to be better prepared for doing business in a global world—communicating, connecting, and exchanging information and ideas with no boundaries or barriers. To benefit from these new communication opportunities, you need to apply the information taught here.

What may be even more important to know is that *not* learning these fundamentals could have a negative impact on your career. I knew several people on the verge of greater success who ultimately did not achieve it, not for lack of talent or knowledge, but because they failed to execute many of the basics. Read the book and you will see why.

In sports, many times teams or individual competitors will fail. When they do, they say they are going "back to the basics." This is necessary in business and life, too. Learn the basics first and avoid many of the failures, and you can travel a direct road to success.

The good news is that it's all up to you.

PART ONE

Professional Practices to Get You Noticed

1. PRESENT THE UNSHAKABLE FACTS

Correct Decisions Depend on Them

I'm starting with this pivotal chapter now because it's the foundation for everything in this book and all decision-making. If you read and apply only what this chapter teaches, you will have an edge in building a successful career.

About ten years into my career, I was working for International Telephone and Telegraph (ITT) in New York City when I received a slick brochure sent to each company employee by Harold Geneen, the legendary chairman and CEO of the first real conglomerate. The eleventh biggest company in the U.S. at the time, ITT's holdings included Avis, O. M. Scott Lawn and Fertilizer (now Scotts Company), Sheraton Hotels, and Hartford Fire and Life Insurance Company (now The Hartford), to name a few. At one of his management meetings, a senior executive of a major division had presented a significant recommendation that was discovered to have been based on "shaky" information that was more fiction than fact.

Infuriated, Geneen immediately wrote a lengthy memo that had become the brochure sitting on my desk. It was sent to every employee in the corporation, some 100,000 people all over the world. His message was simple but powerful: you cannot reach a good decision and course of action unless it is founded on facts. The histories of business and the military abound with disasters caused by a weak base of information that was not factual.

While the business world has certainly changed in many ways, the fundamentals are still as vital for success as they were when Geneen outlined them in 1965. The following is excerpted from the document:

MEMO

Yesterday we put in a long, hard-driving meeting, mostly seeking the "facts" on which easy management decisions could then be made. I think the important conclusion to be drawn is simple.

There is no word in the English language that more strongly conveys the intent of incontrovertibility—i.e., "final and reliable reality"—than the word **fact.**

However, no word is more honored by its breach in actual usage. For example, there are and we saw yesterday:

"Apparent facts"
"Assumed facts"
"Reported facts"
"Hoped-for facts"

"Facts" so labeled and accepted as facts—and many others of similar derivation! In most cases, these were not the "facts" at all. In many cases of daily life, this point may not be too important. But in the areas of management momentum and decisions, it is all-important! Whole trains of events and decisions for an entire management can be put in motion in the wrong direction—with inevitable loss of money, time, and morale—by one "unfactual fact" accepted by or submitted by you, however unintentional.

The highest art of professional management requires the literal ability to "smell" a **real fact** from all others—and moreover to have the temerity, intellectual curiosity, guts and/or plain impoliteness, if necessary, to be sure that what you do have is indeed what we call an **unshakeable fact.**

That is the kind of fact material we have to deal in. And, as a member of the team, it is the only kind you can accept or submit. Our management team has to rely on each member exercising the greatest care in this respect as to the material he or she submits for the team's common use.

So let me invite you and at the same time insist that you now become a "connoisseur" of all these kinds of facts—so that you can tell a "genuine snapping turtle" from the others, and so that you can learn to force to the surface and deal only with **unshakeable facts** in the future.

Effective immediately, I want every report specifically, directly and bluntly to state at the beginning a summary containing the following facts in this order:

1. A clear, short statement of the actions recommended.

2. A brief summary of what the problem really is.

3. The reasoning and the figures, where necessary for clarity and perspective, to understand the basis of the reasoning and judgment areas leading to this recommendation.

4. A brief personal statement by the writer expressing any further personal opinion, his degree of confidence, and any other questions that he has in this respect.

Obviously, to make this kind of direct, clear judgment statement, one must first do hard, crisp thinking and

(memo continued)

adequate homework. Otherwise, we will get a continuation of vague general statements and reports, which indicate no clear position or basis for any, taken by the writer. In the future this kind of indefinite statement and report will be subject to review with the author, and action will be taken on this point alone.

Let me add that there is nothing serious about an occasional wrong conclusion. We should be trained as a group to detect and refute most of these. However, there is a lot of wasted time involved in vague reports, which reflect lack of judgment or homework, and in this direction lies perpetual mediocrity. Let's have none of this!

So, good luck, and start now. But always ask: **Is it a fact?** And, more important: Is it an **"unshakeable fact?"**

Harold S. Geneen

Harold S. Geneen
Chairman and Chief Executive

P.S. No matter what you think is a fact, try "shaking" it to be sure!

P.P.S. Send this message down the line."

I have never forgotten this message because it made so much sense. I had the experience a few years later to attend several of Harold Geneen's management meetings when our company, one of many within the ITT conglomerate, was presenting our business plan to him and his top echelon of executives. It was one of the most intimidating scenes I have ever witnessed.

Picture a room large enough to accommodate about one hundred people all seated around an arrangement of large tables organized in a semicircle in front of the Geneen team. Geneen's side represented about fifty people and the presenting companies about fifty people. To further emphasize the size of this gathering, there were three overhead projectors positioned so that everyone could see the overhead slides at the same time.

My boss was a confident young executive named Herb Kolber. During his presentation, Geneen referred to him as Hank (Herb later told me he didn't have the nerve to correct him but was glad he at least had the first letter correct) and asked, "Would you please show me the basis for the conclusion you just presented?" Herb paused and said, "Mr. Geneen, if you can wait a few minutes, I have an overhead in my presentation that will answer your question." There was total silence because no one ever put Geneen off. Geneen nodded his head and Herb continued with his presentation until he came to the overhead that answered the question. When he finished his explanation, Geneen looked at Herb, smiled, and said, "Young man, it's a good thing you had the right overhead and right answer." There was another brief silence, and then someone laughed nervously, and the whole place, relieved there had been no massacre, erupted in laughter.

You cannot be right if you lack the necessary factual information. Allow me another story to show how damaging the wrong information can be.

I was living and working in Rio de Janeiro, Brazil, for ITT. At our office, we had a young boy whose job was to go from office to office all day long bringing coffee to anyone who wanted a cup. One day a few of the women in the office complained that they were missing valuables from their purses. It was promptly concluded that the young boy who delivered coffee was the thief. After all, he was the only one who regularly went into all our offices. Our chief financial officer, a Brazilian named Felix Prel, discussed the conclusion with us and decided to call in the police, a sure end to this boy's immediate future because he would have no way to prove his innocence. While Felix was on the telephone, one of our accounting clerks came running into the office and announced that a few of his fellow workers had caught two young thieves who had come into the office around lunchtime to steal valuables. They were apprehended and turned over to the police, exonerating the boy just in time. The consequences of jumping to conclusions without having all the facts would have destroyed this boy's future. This has stayed indelibly in my mind.

To get the facts often seems so difficult. No doubt they are available, but the users can distort and slant them to meet their own objectives. In business, I believe the problem is likely to be a failure to dig deep enough to get the facts. The reason is usually the haste to put together recommendations for someone else who is also under time pressure. Shortcuts are taken and the due diligence—a complete investigation— for facts is not thorough.

Under Geneen, the constant pressure to dig deep for the facts and to be right showed me how significant real facts are to effective decision making. Common sense, which is often overlooked, is as important in business as in everyday life.

REMEMBER THIS

You cannot make the correct decision without hard facts. Too often people believe they have the facts when they don't, and the results can be damaging to the company and individuals.

"Mistakes are a fact of life. It is the response to error that counts."
—*Nikki Giovanni*

"Comment is free, but facts are sacred."
—*C. P. Scott*

"The first precept was never to accept a thing as true until I knew it as such without a single doubt."
—*René Descartes*

---

2. USE INFORMATION TO REACH GOOD CONCLUSIONS

Gather It, Analyze It, and Make a Plan to Take Action

For many years, the military intelligence agency has relied on a system to create usable intelligence during times of war. Since my time in the U.S. Air Force, I have used this process, a valid and practical way to study a situation and reach good, solid decisions.

The system involves six steps as follows:

1. COLLECT INFORMATION

In the military, this can mean interrogating prisoners, spies, or witnesses; capturing documents; breaking code; or debriefing your own people such as troops and air crews. In business, you must diligently look everywhere for information and facts; collect information from people, reports, documents, and even the media.

2. COLLATE IT

Put the pieces together to tell a story and be sure to fill in the blanks.

3. ANALYZE AND INTERPRET IT

Take all the collated information and determine what story it is telling. What interpretations can be drawn from the information? How confident are you that your conclusion is correct?

4. SEARCH FOR CONCLUSIONS ABOUT WHAT IT MEANS

Can valid decisions be developed from this information or do you need more? Can you rely on your analysis to direct people to some course of action? How will you evaluate the conclusions reached? Is there a course of action with a high probability of success?

5. COMMUNICATE IT TO THE RIGHT PEOPLE

Forward the conclusions to the right people. This alone is a start toward action.

6. EXECUTE AND FOLLOW THROUGH

After the decisions resulting from the analysis are communicated to the right people, they must be executed. Knowing something without taking action is rarely productive. A detailed schedule of the actions to be accomplished is essential. Once it is executed, there must be follow-through to measure the results.

The military and business worlds both share a need for information in order to reach the right decisions and then take appropriate actions. The information has to be factual to be of value. Once the information is obtained, it must be properly reviewed in order to be worthwhile. Often there is an urgency with time as a major factor.

Back in the late 1960s, ITT, under Harold Geneen, was aggressively acquiring companies and building the largest conglomerate at that time.

Acquisitions are always risky because not all the facts about a company are readily available. Often you must work hard to find them. Without the facts and without a system to examine and validate them, you are liable to make the wrong decisions. One venture that demonstrates the consequences of not starting with the right information and not testing it adequately relates to the construction of a new plant in Canada for Rayonier, a then-recently-acquired forest products ITT company. The new plant was to be built near a forest of millions of acres of timber and would process wood into cellulose. All the facts were examined, checked, and verified, but there was one important fact not uncovered: no one knew that the extreme cold would prevent the trees from growing more than three inches in diameter. The economics of simply cutting these skinny trees and transporting them to the plant would not support a profitable business. No one had ever actually seen these trees before the multimillion-dollar expansion was started. Not enough information had been collected and put through a process to reach valid decisions.

In many companies, the collection phase has been elevated to a science; they have a group that deals with competitive intelligence. This group seeks feedback from their sales and field reps, who hear about other companies and know reps from other companies. They know how to obtain information from their customers and their competitors' customers and from trade journals, company reports, online, and even purchased industry reports, especially useful in terms of the marketplace and new products. This vital group performs the intelligence cycle and can produce valuable information. A disciplined approach like this can help to guarantee a valid conclusion and productive course of action.

All that I've said about the military intelligence cycle fits very well with chapter 1, "Present the Unshakable Facts," because you must start the process with unshakable facts. Whether you play a supporting role or a key one, are recommending a new copier or a new product line, combining facts with the intelligence cycle should allow you to reach the right decisions. The quality of your work and the accuracy of your facts and conclusions will always determine your progress to the corner office. Be logical, correct, and keep it as simple as possible.

REMEMBER THIS

The military intelligence cycle is a logical way to gather and examine information, to search for facts, and reach conclusions that can be productively used to make decisions.

"The great aim of education is not knowledge but action."
— Herbert Spencer

"You can never get all the facts from just one newspaper, and unless you have all the facts, you cannot make proper judgments about what is going on."
— Harry S. Truman

"It's no use saying, 'We are doing our best.' You have got to succeed in doing what is necessary."
—Winston Churchill

3. TACKLE PROBLEMS HEAD-ON

Simplify by Looking at Them in Pieces

Problems can come to you in many forms—people-related, operations, marketing, planning, logistics, and more. The solution for all of these comes from simplifying and breaking each down into smaller pieces for better understanding and analysis. This new organization of facts can then be logically reviewed for solutions and conclusions.

Once you can figure out what the problem is, there are many ways to go about solving it.

For instance, I see things much easier and can plan more effectively when I can diagram the issue or problem. I rely on my yellow pad or a white board where I can draw and diagram a list of known facts or a flow chart. This works especially well, even if I am working with one person and want to tie down key points. I am drawn to charts and graphs because they let me break out the pieces and prevent over complicating matters.

I learned another problem-solving tool one time while I was meeting with the Boston Consulting Group, a top-flight organization with sixty offices around the world. **One of their associates told me about his simple but effective way to get answers: Asking "why?" about five times. The theory is that by the fifth why you will probably have collected all there is to know. With each why, you dig deeper. It is a very powerful way to collect all the information you need to help solve a problem.**

The following story, whether it is true or just an amusing tale, shows how you can peel away the layers and get to the bottom of an issue. This was an e-mail with no known author sent to me by a friend. For the purposes of this exercise, I would assume it is fiction.

The U.S. standard railroad gauge (width between the two rails) is 4 feet, 8.5 inches. That's an exceedingly odd number. **Why** *was that gauge used? Because that's the way they built them in England, and the U.S. railroads were built by English expatriates.*

Why *did the English build them like that? Because the first rail lines were built by the same people who built the pre-railroad tramways, and that's the gauge they used.*

Why *did "they" use that gauge then? Because the people who built the tramway used the same jigs and tools that they used for building wagons which used that wheel spacing.*

Okay! **Why** *did the wagons have that particular odd wheel spacing? Well, if they tried to use any other spacing, the wagon wheels would break on some of the old, long-distance roads through England, because that was the spacing of the wheel ruts.*

So **who** *built those old rutted roads? The first long-distance roads in England (and the rest of Europe) were built by Imperial Rome for its legions. The roads have been used ever since.*

And **why** *the ruts in the roads? Roman war chariots first formed the initial ruts, which everyone else had to match for fear of destroying their wagon wheels. Because the chariots were made for (or by) Imperial Rome, they were all alike in the matter of wheel spacing.*

The United States standard railroad gauge of 4 feet, 8.5 inches derives from the original specification for an Imperial Roman chariot. Specifications and bureaucracies live forever. So the next time you are handed a specification and wonder what horse's ass came up with it, you may be exactly right, because the Imperial Roman war chariots were made just wide enough to accommodate the back ends of two war horses. Thus, we have the answer to the original question.

Now the extraterrestrial twist to the story . . .

When we see a space shuttle sitting on its launch pad, there are two big booster rockets attached to the sides of the main fuel tank. These are solid rocket boosters, or SRBs. The SRBs are made by Thiokol at their factory in Utah. The engineers who designed the SRBs might have preferred to make them a bit fatter, but the SRBs had to be shipped by train from the factory to the launch site.

The railroad line from the factory had to run through a tunnel in the mountains. The SRBs had to fit through that tunnel. The tunnel is slightly wider than the railroad track, and the railroad track is about as wide as two horses' behinds.

So, if this story is true, the major design feature of what is arguably the world's most advanced transportation system was determined over two thousand years ago by the width of a horse's ass.

REMEMBER THIS

Problems can be complex, but solving them can be simplified if you look at them in pieces. Whether you use flow charts, diagrams, or ask questions that dig deeper for more facts, keep your efforts organized and logical.

"It takes courage to push yourself to places you have never been before . . . to test your limits . . . to break through barriers."

— Unknown

"I think and think for months and years. Ninety-nine times, the conclusion is false. The hundredth time I am right."

— Albert Einstein

"Millions saw the apple fall, but Newton was the only one who asked why."

— Bernard Baruch

4. COMMUNICATE CONFIDENTLY

In Speech and Writing, Be Clear and Interesting

Y ou communicate every day, whether in a one-on-one situation, a presentation to many, or a report. You can't avoid communication, so it is to your advantage to do it well.

Take the time to learn how to speak effectively and to write clearly and concisely. Whether speaking or writing, make it interesting.

Put yourself in the other person's place. Would you understand you? Are you taking for granted a level of understanding that your audience may not have? For example, sometimes computer techies explain something to a non-tech user assuming a level of knowledge non-techies don't have. Keep your explanation as simple and logical as possible. Start at the beginning and don't assume everyone knows what you know.

Be a teacher. Good teachers are valuable and actually become better teachers when they learn from their students. Be factual, interesting, and thorough. Even if you have good information, your story and recommendations may go down the drain if your audience just doesn't get it.

Become known as someone who can present information clearly and logically. How many times in the course of a day do you find people giving you incomplete information? You have to ask questions over and over to get the whole story. Take your time when you are speaking. Notice that the best speakers slow the pace so you understand and catch all of the words and thoughts.

Use proper grammar because your image is at stake. If you know that your grammar is poor, then learn and correct the obvious mistakes. There are many good basic books available and courses you can take at a community college or online. If you are in a key situation trying to get your message to an important person, you could kill your chances with obvious grammatical mistakes. I had a veteran salesman tell me once that he wanted to keep me "post-dated." I said, "Do you mean posted?" He laughed and said, "You know what I mean." As effective as he was in sales, I had to be selective about assigning him to represent the department or the company at meetings.

Whatever you do, let your speech and writing express your personality. You will do better by being yourself because it is more genuine and believable.

An important area in this whole arena of communications is the use of voice mail, a really great tool. Always leave your phone number. Even if you know the party knows your number. He may get your message while traveling and be unable to easily find it. Also, speak slowly and clearly. Have you noticed how frequently people rush through their phone number, causing you to replay the message? This seemingly small point is all a part of communicating effectively and ultimately impacts your image. When you rush through your phone number, it tells the party that you think the call may be a bother for him so you want to get it done quickly. It's like when a presenter rushes through her charts or graphs; she conveys the idea that they are unimportant or that she believes the audience is really not interested.

We all know how important and useful cell phones are, and how annoying and disruptive when used without regard for other people. During a meeting, common sense would tell you not to make calls or leave the ringer on. If an urgent call is expected, you might set the phone to vibrate, and then leave the meeting to answer or to make a call. If you do use the vibration feature, keep the phone off the tabletop to prevent the disrupting and embarrassing rattle when a call comes through. Although this is all pretty basic, this etiquette is often not followed.

Another key business tool often misused is e-mail. Here are seven guidelines to keep in mind:

1. Use a clear and descriptive subject line. Be sure to change the subject line if it no longer matches the current exchange.

2. Write concisely.

3. Watch what you say. Tone can easily be misunderstood in an email and cause unnecessary conflicts. Always remember your email can readily be forwarded to someone else.

4. Don't use email as a tool to show everyone how busy you are.

5. Copy only those who really need to see the email instead of copying everyone you can think of.

6. Review your email and use spell check before sending. A missing word can change the meaning dramatically.

7. Realize when your message should be delivered face to face or over the phone instead of email. This applies to difficult conversations as well as ones that could be handled more effectively with direct contact. If you want a written record of the conversation, simply follow up with an email later.

Finally, your communication style and technique can overshadow what you are saying. It helps to understand your audience whether it consists of one person or three hundred people. How should you approach them and present your message? Be as clear as you can with a touch of humor and wit. Never read your message. Know your message well and then learn to use notes effectively to present it. Your body language, eyes, posture, and presence tell a whole story. When you are in a conversation, use your skills as a good listener. Without doing this, you will be in a vacuum with no real exchange of information. Because communication, both verbal and written, is so important, it's worth investing in some help—such as a seminar, a teacher, or some good reading—so you can learn to excel at it. It's well worth the effort.

REMEMBER THIS

You must communicate to succeed. Speaking and writing skills are essential. Learn what you do right and what you do wrong; then, if necessary, get some help. Do whatever you can to be the best communicator.

*"Communication skills are the lifeblood of a successful life . . .
if you plan on spending any time there."*
— Doug Firebaugh

"Colors fade, temples crumble, empires fall, but wise words endure."
— Edward Thorndike

*"The rewards in business go to the man who
does something with an idea."*
— William Benton

5. Don't Try to Go It Alone

Support and Cooperation Will Get the Job Done

Every successful executive is surrounded with the best cast of executives and managers. Oftentimes you will see these supporting people move out on their own and succeed at the highest levels in other companies.

Some companies are known for the future executives and CEOs they develop. They hire the best, delegate and train the best, promote the best, and then track their performance. They develop a mutual trust and retain the best.

When Harold Geneen ran ITT, he had an office of the president staffed by five executive vice presidents. This stable group had no turnover, and although there was turnover down the line, Geneen could always count on this group of five and a few other executives. Geneen was able to take ITT from $765 million in sales to $22 billion in the eighteen years he was chairman and CEO. He knew that in spite of his energy and skills, he could not do it alone.

Remembering you can't do it alone will help you progress in your company and your career. Networks are essential because rarely can you accomplish anything without people to assist you. Everyone needs a network. They will vary in size and talent, but most people want to help and know that they will need help at some point, too. This also extends to people who are outside of your company. Whether you seek advice and information on a work project or for a personal endeavor, realize that eventually everyone will find themselves in the same position. It's also common knowledge that most of the best recruiting comes through networks.

At the beginning of your career, start your network with your classmates and favorite professors. At your first job, get to know people throughout the company, from the mailroom to the CEO. Resist the urge to only talk to people you know when attending company parties, your spouse's company parties, seminars, and tradeshows; make a point to talk to at least three people you don't know at such events. Consider joining the company's softball league or going to lunch with those in your department.

Other important components of your network are mentors. More than likely, you will find your mentor in your own company. Mentors are the people respected for their accomplishments and wisdom. Most people are flattered when you ask for their advice and insights; however, you should always evaluate their advice and use common sense. They can develop an interest in you and your career and will act like coaches trying to help you succeed.

Mentors often have protégés they are grooming for higher positions, maybe even their own. Remember that good executives strive to have a backup who is being prepared to step up. One of the most critical tasks that a top-level person has is to have a replacement for himself or herself.

Find the right people, recruit them, train them, and retain the best. Build the right team and success will follow. In contrast, companies with high executive turnover will always be in trouble. Changing top-level people almost always results in a ripple effect as each layer of managers under the top is also changed. A new president brings in a few trusted lieutenants and each of them does the same. This is repeated down the line, resulting in maybe fifteen or twenty changes or more. The same effect can be generated even by lower-level people coming into an organization and the same ripple effect is started.

During my nine years at Burger King Corporation as the executive vice president and chief administrative officer, I worked for several different presidents and CEOs. Burger King's mediocre growth at that time, compared to some of their competition, showed how difficult it is to develop a program and consistently implement a plan with so many high-level changes.

Try to retain your best people and avoid the ripple effect often caused by key replacements. If you are placed in a position of responsibility, whether it is at the top or a few levels below, you cannot do that job without competent and trusted support.

Never be afraid of placing people in your organization who have talent, skills, and intelligence that may exceed yours. They will help you to succeed. Recognize them and reward them. Develop mutual trust and respect and you won't be disappointed.

In order to seed your organization with the best people, you must find and cultivate the winners. If those people are not in your organization already, take the time to choose the best candidate. Too often recruiting is rushed.

Usually, someone recommended to you by respected friends or associates is likely to be a better choice, but the interviewing should be no less rigorous than with someone who comes to you through any other source.

In addition to having the right talent, knowledge, experience, and skills, be sure the candidate's character and chemistry mix well with the rest of your organization. Avoid hiring shadows of yourself, as many do. You need a mix of talent and personalities to get healthy and diversified opinions. Interviews that are well prepared and social events such as lunch, dinner, or going to a ball game can be very revealing. Get to know this person deeper than their resumé or your first impressions. The candidate's value system and attitude are extremely important.

You can't change someone's personality, and if you believe the chemistry could be wrong or the person is not coachable, be very cautious. Make an extra effort to know these things and use personality tests to learn more.

Hire slowly, and when justified, fire quickly. If you find that you hired the wrong person, then you must act fast. Waiting probably will not improve your candidate and will only cause you and the new recruit more problems. Remember, it's your responsibility if you have chosen the wrong candidate. Be fair and professional in how you treat the person. You always want anyone leaving your company to leave on the best terms possible. You want that person to say good things about your company or at least be neutral. You want to avoid as much negativism as possible.

Even with highly talented people, you must provide leadership and direction. Strive to build loyalty; this quality is often absent in today's business environment. Loyalty must be earned on both sides, but it really pays off when it exists.

Don't let good performance go unrecognized. Let that person know that you appreciate their work. This goes a long way, and it is so easy to do. That said, recognition doesn't happen enough. The good performer who is identified will likely do an even better job, constantly looking for recognition and success. It's also true for the average performer. You will get improved performance and a better attitude.

Years later, I still remember one very special reward I got for my work. The president of a company I was with asked me to assist him in writing a strategic plan for the Boy Scouts of America. He sat on their board and knew I had some experience with planning. We worked together, did the plan, presented it, and were recognized for our work with individual plaques. Back at the company, he called me in to his office, said he couldn't have done it without me, and told me to pick any place in the country for an all-expense-paid weekend trip for my family and me. We still talk about that great weekend. My children, twelve and fourteen at the time, had a rare chance for a weekend at a place they might not normally have visited. They also knew that it was because of my performance that I received double recognition. None of us will forget that special trip, and the recognition meant more to me than if it had been a cash award. The president had a well-deserved reputation as a people person and was known for always recognizing performance.

I recently heard this on the radio: "Some will do what you expect, but many will do what you inspect." That message means to me: don't have a workforce that reacts only to your constant vigilance. On the other hand, people will always react favorably to your recognition of their efforts.

A common thread that runs through all of this discussion is the need to be courteous and friendly with all of those you encounter at work. There are many people who are and will continue to be important when you need something done. For example, you may need the mail-room people to stay late to help you with last-minute copying. Or you may need to get in to see the top executive immediately and the executive assistant controls the schedule. How you've always treated them will directly affect their attitude and helpfulness. You get what you give.

REMEMBER THIS

The support and cooperation from the people around you will greatly determine your success. Don't try to go it alone. Use the best talent to brainstorm and help on projects. Delegate and recognize all contributions. Extend your network beyond your normal boundaries.

"The best time to make friends is before you need them."
— Henny Youngman

"You don't manage people; you manage things. You lead people."
— Admiral Grace Hooper

"Each of us has a spark of life inside us, and our highest endeavor ought to be to set that spark off in another."
— Kenny Ausubel

6. TRACK VITAL LIFE SIGNS

Learn What Makes a Company in Your Industry Financially Sound

Allbusinesses have common vital life signs such as sales and profit, with other financial measurements in between.

Each company also has vital life signs specific to that company. Beyond the normal sales and profit figures, there could be measures such as the average loan size, number of late payments, and number of foreclosures on loans. Each company and industry has its own, and you must be familiar with them. You should know the sales of your company, the number of employees, the profitability, and general history. I'm often surprised that people I meet can't tell me the most basic information about their company. Some don't even have an idea. You don't need exact numbers—close is good enough. Knowing the answers shows that you are dedicated and reliable and helps you stand out from your colleagues. I can't stress enough how important this is.

Looking at the vital life signs from another angle, your future could depend on how well your company is doing. Knowing these measurements may help you to predict your future. It helps you to focus more on the ways you can help your company and your own career, too.

When I was with Burger King Corporation, some vital life signs were average sales per restaurant, changes in those sales from the previous year, and average check size compared to the previous year. Others were employee turnover at the restaurant level and restaurant growth in the United States and overseas. If I wasn't tracking these basic numbers,

I could have missed the early signs of success or failure, affecting both the company and myself.

Every industry has its own indicators. Find out what they are in your business and how you can track them. Your interest alone could set you apart from the others, especially if you are new to the company. As a veteran, you are expected to know, and if you don't, you show that either you don't care or you don't think it is important. Either answer is a bad answer. A newer employee can be forgiven but only for a short time. For a new person, knowing is a big plus.

To find out the vital life signs of your company and how to track them, you must ask people at higher levels about the keys to success in your company and industry. Beyond the obvious of sales, profit, and year-to-year growth figures, what are the pieces that make it happen? By knowing these, you will develop an understanding of your business, and this knowledge will improve your performance.

In addition, you will be able to see how your company is competing, especially if you also know the numbers for others in the industry. You often can find these figures on the company's Web site or annual report. It may also give you ideas that can help your company reduce expenses or gain a competitive edge. I remember a new young employee at Burger King who was amazed at the high turnover of employees in the restaurants. Each job had to be filled three times per year. This was, of course, very expensive for the company and led to poor service in the restaurants.

The new employee became so obsessed with this problem that he developed a program of incentives that was eventually introduced to the restaurants, reducing the turnover rate. Needless to say, he made himself a rising star with a strong reputation that led to recognition and a bright future.

Another example of a vital life sign is the design and cost of a product that could have a dramatic effect on a company's performance. In the early '90s, I was president of a small company in Miami called

Contraband Detection International. We had a contract with British Aerospace Securities System in England to market in the United States a high-tech mass spectrometer that could detect explosives and drugs. The machine was extremely accurate and very fast in making the detection and identification. Unfortunately, the machine was too big (10 by 5 by 3 feet), too heavy (2,000 pounds), and too expensive (about $5 million).

Recognizing all these liabilities, we made recommendations to the manufacturer, a Canadian company. The manufacturer was finally able to redesign the machine and make it about half the size of the top of a desk for $300,000. We knew that the Federal Aviation Administration, The Department of Defense, and the Department of Drug Enforcement would all be receptive. At about this same time, the president of the Canadian manufacturing company resigned, and the new president elected not to continue the project, viewing it as too speculative. We'll never know what would have happened with this machine, but its vital life signs were improved for success, even though success didn't come.

Know what is important about your company. What constitutes success and failure? What are the sales, number of employees, and geographic coverage? If you are not knowledgeable, you appear uninformed and uninterested in your company. Knowing details beyond the obvious will allow you to help your company and see trends early enough to make decisions, either to help you in your job or possibly lead you to find another job.

REMEMBER THIS

Knowing the vital life signs of your company and industry is essential. This knowledge will help you to be more effective and be recognized as someone who is on the ball.

"There is no substitute for accurate knowledge.
Know yourself, know your business, know your people."

— Randall Jacobs

"Life is my college."

— Louisa May Alcott

"Get all the advice you can, and you will succeed;
without it you will fail."

— Proverbs 15:22

7. BE AN EAGER LEARNER

The More You Know, the More Valuable You Are

Whether you are underperforming in your job or performing well, you can always be improving. Make a real effort to learn from everything you see and do; watch, ask questions, think, and react.

Your quest to know more should never stop. Your brain needs exercise just as your body does. Keep it active. Be creative and think of new and better ways to do your job. Think about how your company can improve and how you can help.

Ask your supervisor questions. This has a double benefit. You will learn something and also demonstrate an interest that others probably haven't, setting yourself apart.

Learning requires a solid commitment, just like regular exercise, and should be an integral part of your effort to succeed in your career and in your life. You must program it to happen.

After serving in the U.S. Air Force, I was hired by New Jersey Bell Telephone, then a part of AT&T. A friend of mine, who had also served, decided to get his law degree using the G.I. Bill, which offered excellent educational benefits. Because he had a full-time job, he decided to get his education at night. I made the same decision and enrolled at the Rutgers Graduate Business School, studying two nights a week, four hours each night for three years to earn my MBA. It was a difficult task, but I couldn't leave my job to study as a full-time student. I knew that the MBA would be advantageous and would uniquely position me with a select few who had MBAs. My effort was recognized by my supervisor and other key decision makers. Although learning was important, the image I created was just as valuable.

Other options to broaden and deepen your work skills and knowledge include seminars, conferences, and trade organizations' publications and e-newsletters. Your network will also help keep you up to date on the latest trends and technology in your field. In short, learning keeps you marketable.

In addition, you should appear to have a certain level of intellect and curiosity about the world to be considered for many jobs. In the same way you may track sporting events, you must be aware of the newsworthy events, facts, and personalities and able to discuss them. Knowledge of politics, geography, and history also will help you better understand current events.

Certainly, not all education has to be formal, such as going to school, but all learning is recognized and helps you stand out from the crowd. Make learning a top priority. Years of school may have turned you off of education, but the reality is, you were born curious. You can rekindle that innate desire to know more—and earn a reputation as a resource and a problem solver in the process.

REMEMBER THIS

Learn from everything. Your quest to know more should never stop. Know what's important in the local, national, and world news. You will perform your job better and brighten up your life.

"If a man empties his purse into his head, no one can take it away from him. An investment of knowledge always pays the best interest."
— Benjamin Franklin

*"Intelligent people want to learn
but stupid people are satisfied with ignorance."*
— Proverbs 15:14

"The ultimate competitive advantage lies in an organization's ability to learn and rapidly transform learning into action."
— Jack Welch

8. ASK FOR WHAT YOU WANT

Don't Expect Rewards to Come Automatically

I've learned over the years, in almost every job, that promotions, rewards, and good things don't necessarily come to you just because of your performance. Although employees oftentimes are rewarded for their contributions, this doesn't happen all the time. There are times when you must ask for what you believe you deserve, and this may include raises and bonuses. You could open the eyes of your boss, who may then decide that you should be rewarded. **If you can present your situation well and demonstrate your job performance, you may get what you want. If you don't ask, you may not succeed or not succeed soon enough.**

This doesn't mean that you should con your way into promotions and develop a reputation for being a politician. Certainly, putting someone in a job he can't do is unfair to that person, to the boss, and to the company. A good supervisor will know whether you are ready or not, but may be preoccupied with other priorities and problems and isn't thinking about you and your future. There likely will be a time when you can and should present your request and ask for what you want.

I remember traveling on a plane with my CEO to a meeting. We were seated together and had more than three hours to talk. I believed we needed a chief administration officer and felt I could do that job. I took the opportunity to present my ideas to him and suggested that I could do this job. We discussed it in detail, and by the time we landed, I had convinced him to create the job and give me this new position.

Another request you may want to approach your boss about is an opportunity to attend a conference or seminar that you feel will help you and your company. In this situation, chances are that you would be able to go if you asked, but you won't if you don't.

"Ask and you may receive" can apply to many things in life. Although you may not get what you want when you ask, you are less likely to get what you want if you don't ask.

REMEMBER THIS

If your request is fair and practical, there is nothing wrong with asking for it. It happens all the time in sales when you ask for an order or when you pitch your services to a client. In any case, asking will improve your chances—and not asking could mean it won't happen.

"If you expect nothing, you are apt to be surprised. You'll get it."
— Malcolm S. Forbes

"Things turn out best for people who make the best out of the way things turn out."
— Art Linkletter

"Life is a series of sales situations, and the answer is NO if you don't ask."
— Patricia Fripp

---

9. PACKAGE YOURSELF FOR SALE

Present Your Work and Yourself in the Best Light Possible

A friend of mine, a well-known veteran marketing and advertising strategist, told me once that "perception is reality." It's what the buyer perceives that is real to the buyer. The same is true in business and in your career. It's how people perceive you that is real. It's up to you to position your strengths and minimize your weaknesses. Show your best side and develop a reputation that you want people to believe.

You are known by your work, your presentation, your personality, and your reputation. Try to package all of them to best present yourself to those who count.

Consider the following points:

YOUR PACKAGING

Good information can be hidden or buried in a document that appears to be unprofessionally made, cheap, or at best mediocre. For example, a local ad agency sent me a brochure with good information, but the brochure was printed on cheap paper. The color was drab, and the whole look was unappealing. This was from an ad agency trying to sell me their services. How could they represent us if they couldn't even present their own story in an appealing package? Needless to say, I had no interest in associating my work with theirs.

This holds true for any work you do—reports, letters, or proposals.

It must look good, be professionally done, and catch the reader's eye and interest. Color is always an eye-catcher. Use charts, diagrams, highlights, and headings. Ideas get lost when not presented well.

Patience plays a role here. Don't rush work out that is not of high quality. Be sure you take the time to present your work well. Many a good idea or proposal fails or goes nowhere because the presenter didn't have the patience to put together a strong story or present it logically. Instead, he rushed through the story and didn't sell it. On the other hand, there is a fine line between taking the time to do it right but not taking too much time. You still must fit your creativity within a time line.

YOUR REPUTATION

Be known as reliable, responsive, and honest. These are traits that are under your control. Other characteristics such as creativity and high intelligence may not be available to you. This is why you must build on your strengths. Be a volunteer. When a job needs to be done, step forward, and take it. There are others who won't volunteer because they don't want the additional responsibility. Their lack of initiative is your gain.

YOUR PERSONALITY AND APPEARANCE

Your personality is actually already established, but you can improve parts of it. Try to understand yourself and seek other opinions to help you. Know your strengths and weaknesses. Take some tests that measure them. This does not have to be expensive. Two tests that come to mind are the Personality Inventory by Myers and Briggs and the Hogan Personality Inventory. Both are available through career coaches and online.

A few obvious weaknesses can be corrected. If you are unusually shy or, on the other side of the scale, too aggressive, you may be able to become more balanced. If part of your personality is a career problem, then I suggest you seriously consider getting professional help, an invaluable resource for promoting self-knowledge.

Appearance, on the other hand, is more controllable. Learn your weaknesses and work on them. Obvious weaknesses such as being poorly dressed or needing a haircut are easily corrected. In addition, being excessively overweight can detract from your image and can limit your opportunities for success.

While there are things you can control and work on, you must know what they are to develop a plan to improve yourself. Some may be serious issues, but the subjects I have described here are probably correctable. You simply must take the initiative.

YOUR PRESENTATIONS

Careful preparation of a key presentation or speech is worth the time and effort to guarantee you are perceived positively. It's always wise to rehearse and become familiar with the material and to time the length of your presentation.

A few things I have learned along the way:

• Don't read it. Use notes instead and maintain eye contact with your audience.

• Speak clearly and slow it down. Give people a chance to follow you and absorb your message.

• Check the sound system and any projection or computer equipment in advance to allow time for adjustments before your presentation.

I also would recommend videotaping your rehearsal. It's easy to do. Put the camera on a tripod or platform and turn it on. You'll be able to see and hear everything the audience will—your body language, eye contact, and voice level. A few hours invested could pay multiple dividends in how you are perceived.

YOUR REGRETS

Have you ever left a meeting or a discussion and said, "I wish I had said this," or "I should have shown them that"? You realize you have wasted a good opportunity to promote yourself. It's okay. Learn from this and rest assured there will always be another time when you can shine and impress. One really good appearance, doing or saying something really important or significant, can make up for the previous lackluster times. But while there is always another chance, try to strike as early in your career as possible to make your reputation known and visible.

You may also experience a time when you say the wrong thing. You may, for example, use words that are critical of an associate and immediately regret it. In an effort to be clever, your words may not have been appropriate. In cases where the advice "think before you speak" would come too late, it's time to skillfully clarify your words as diplomatically as you can. It's better to face up to it right there than to let it brew. Humor may help.

BEING A FRANCHISE PLAYER

You know that in sports the key player is considered a franchise player. The reward is in money and security, such as a no-trade clause and long-term contract. In business you can also be a franchise player by being better than your associates. You will be singled out, rewarded, and protected. Sometimes it doesn't take a whole lot to stand out. A word of caution, though—you should maintain good relationships with your associates and not take actions at their expense to achieve your success. Believe me, such behavior will be noticed and work against you.

If you successfully execute many of the tips and tools in this book, you will stand out. Look around you. What do you see in your associates? Do they execute the basics in their jobs? Does your boss recognize your contributions and see the difference between you and your associates?

YOUR STRENGTHS AND WEAKNESSES / LIKES AND DISLIKES

In addition to examining your strengths and weaknesses, you should match them up with your likes and dislikes. If you are strong in an area and also like to do that job, you are much more likely to succeed, in part because of your obvious enthusiasm for the work.

If you look around yourself, you will see that it isn't the most diffi-cult task to stand out if you package yourself to be professional and unique. Use some of the recommendations made here and you will multiply your chances of being recognized. You'll find out there are a lot of average and mediocre coworkers who won't extend themselves. Their ambition is likely less than yours. Your success will depend on how much you go for what you want.

REMEMBER THIS

You must sell yourself and your work. Packaging it all successfully is how you do it. Perception is reality, so take your best step forward. It is no small effort, but you must take the time to do it right.

"Good business leaders create a vision, articulate the vision, passionately own the vision, and relentlessly drive it to completion."
— John Welch

"Life isn't about finding yourself. Life is about creating yourself."
— George Bernard Shaw

"People make the decisions about you in the first ten seconds after they meet you for the first time. Do whatever it takes to make those first ten seconds positive ones."
— Tom Hopkins

---

10. PLAN YOUR CAREER

Keep Your Skills Marketable

If you are just starting to seek a career, obvious questions include "What do I want to do?" and "What do I enjoy doing and how can I apply this to a source of income and a career?" If you are past the starting point and in the market with a job and career, the question can still be "Am I doing what I really like"? If so, does it seem to have a career path? If not, ask yourself, "Why am I still doing it?"

There are some lucky people who have career goals early in their lives, but many more don't know and prepare themselves with a broad, general education that will probably get them a good job with a company. Although it takes a certain amount of luck to end up at the right company in a department doing a job that you enjoy, planning your career can help ensure you'll arrive where you want to be. Here are several tips to help you get there.

STICK TO WHAT YOU KNOW—and know your own business. Much has been said and written about this. Books such as Al Ries's *Focus* (HarperBusiness) have described the pitfalls of going too wide and getting out of your real expertise. This is as true for companies as for individuals. It helps if you can get positioned early in your career to learn about an industry and be focused rather than to be a generalist.

There are a few top executives, such as the late Harold Geneen of ITT fame, who would not agree with this. He felt that a good manager could manage anything. In some cases, this is true, but years of experience in the same kind of business can be a real strength.

Wherever you end up, you must manage your career. Don't leave it to chance.

BECOME, AND STAY, MARKETABLE. The days are over when you could carve out a career with a single company. Today you must have market-able skills that you can sell to many companies. This includes building on your strengths and minimizing your weaknesses. Try to change weaknesses into strengths or at least neutralize them. Even if you stay with one company for many years, chances are you will have new bosses along the way or the company may be sold. In both cases, your skills and knowledge will be evaluated as though you are a potential new hire; therefore, you must be marketable.

To avoid the situation where you have been downsized with no place to go, you must be prepared with broader job skills. Think and learn now, not later. Times are changing, and you can't stay narrow in your job. Remember the skill-building suggestions we discussed in chapter 7, "Be an Eager Learner."

BE PREPARED FOR THE CHOICES THAT YOU MAY BE OFFERED AND THE FORKS IN THE ROAD. We all come to them—what job to take, which city to live in, even who to marry—whether it be by choice or by chance. Each will lead you in a different direction. Try to know ahead of time which road or choice to follow. That said, there are times when you should deviate from a plan and get out of your comfort zone. For example, a friend of mine had just graduated high in his class from Cornell University and had multiple job interviews. At one interview, he noticed an open spot on the schedule for a job that specified only MBAs. He asked if he could be interviewed even though he did not have an MBA because there was the open spot in the schedule. Reluctantly, they agreed. His interview went so well that he was offered the position. He has continued to be successful and is now a vice president on a fast track. He stepped out of his comfort zone, deviated from his plan, and took a major step forward.

ESTABLISH A LINK WITH SOMEONE WHO IS, OR WHO IS LIKELY TO BE, SUCCESSFUL. This connection can help you enormously and also help your colleague. Friendships, relationships, and ties have great value, as we discussed previously. When people succeed, they like to take trusted friends with them as support. It's always more enjoyable to work closely with a friend. Even if you are the beneficiary of a relationship, you must perform well. Friendship goes only so far. If you aren't a quality performer and don't add value, you could hurt your sponsor. I have seen cases where someone who was brought along fizzled or failed somewhere along the way. A relationship will give you an opportunity, but without your solid contribution, you become a liability.

LEARN TO RECOGNIZE THE SIGNS OF FAILURE AS EARLY AS POSSIBLE, whether they show up in your job performance, your career path, your company, or your industry. You must see them and analyze them.

Over the years, I've seen examples of this in every one of these categories. Sometimes steps were taken to avert disaster, but many times no action was taken even though the evidence was obvious.

In most cases, things probably aren't going to get better. What you see and feel is likely to be true. This is the time to examine the facts, make some decisions, and then act. Be sure, though, that you do have unshakable facts before you put changes in motion.

There's likely to come a time when you will be out of work. In this world we live in, where corporate downsizing has become common and global competition and outsourcing are also factors, you must be prepared for another job.

If you find yourself in this distressing position, remember that you are certainly not alone and that thousands have passed this way before you. Many became re-employed, and some of them eventually became successful and also became well known. Regardless of how you become unemployed, you should regard it as a temporary situation and use it as an opportunity to reassess your goals, your plan, your skills, and your current financial and personal situation. Ask yourself if you want to continue doing the same kind of work or if it is time to make a change.

If you want to make a change, are you prepared in terms of your skills, education, and financial stability? How much do you really want to change your direction and are you willing and able to take this path?

Seek advice from your friends, family, and network. You could embark on the most important and rewarding milestone of your working career. If you decide that you want to do more of the same kind of work, it could be easier unless the career field is shrinking and becoming a dead end. It is time to think, not panic, maintain a positive attitude, and present yourself as a confident person ready for a new challenge.

In summary, you must plan your career instead of letting circumstances be the basis for your direction. Think through your strengths and weaknesses coupled with your likes and dislikes. Seek help to do this as soon as you can, but better late than never. Chart your course for education, jobs, companies, and industries that best fit your profile. Learn skills that are marketable and broadly useful, not just skills that might fit a particular job in a particular company or industry. Planning combined with the tips and tools described in this book will help you map a career you will enjoy and that will give you success.

REMEMBER THIS

It is up to you to plan your career and the steps needed to be successful. The earlier the better, but a late start is better than no start. Be valuable and marketable wherever you are and keep your horizons broad. Your networks are important but are not a substitute for having goals.

"The person who makes a success of living is the one who sees his goal steadily and aims for it unswervingly. That is dedication."
— Cecil B. DeMille

"The people who get on in this world are the people who get up and look for the circumstances they want, and if they can't find them, make them."
— George Bernard Shaw

"You control your future, your destiny. What you think about comes about. By recording your dreams and goals on paper, you set in motion the process of becoming the person you most want to be. Put your future in good hands—your own."
— Mark Victor Hansen

11. PREPARE FOR MEETINGS

This is the Most Important Thing That Can Set You Apart

We would all agree that meetings and planning are extremely essential to our businesses. Yet to have productive meetings and useful planning, we shouldn't forget the value of pre-meetings and pre-planning.

Pre-meetings are merely preparations for an effective meeting. While this may seem obvious, in my experience, this step often doesn't happen.

To prepare, think about why you are meeting and know the issues. You may find yourself busy and overwhelmed with work. You might see a meeting listed on your calendar coming up and do a quick mental review or check some papers quickly. Usually this isn't enough. My advice is to schedule prep time well in advance of the meeting and, if necessary, take work home with you. Don't jeopardize your career by being unprepared and unknowledgeable about the issues.

If you are going to a meeting with another department or another company, you must know ahead of time what your goals are, and what you are willing to do or not do and give up or not give up. In other words, have your own pre-meeting to be properly prepared for the meeting. Many issues can't be decided in a meeting without an understanding of what your acceptable positions are.

Other vital basics: know what charts and graphs to use; know what you want to say; and have the documents you want to distribute with the right number of copies ready. Don't fumble and waste time at the meeting.

In the role of the chairperson, be sure there is an agenda that is specific and clearly understood. Be known as a person who runs a well-organized and productive meeting.

Let people know that they had better be prepared and be contributors in a professional environment.

A word about meetings: when one or more people are late to a meeting, the meeting has to be delayed either while waiting for them or while the late ones are briefed when they arrive. Delays of any sort make a meeting appear to be unprofessional, set the wrong tone, and cost the company time and money. I remember when I was in the U.S. Air Force and the base commander had staff meetings every morning at 6:00 a.m. He regularly arrived at 5:59 a.m. At 6:00 a.m., the door was closed and locked behind him, and late arrivals were locked out. Their absence was conspicuous and, needless to say, they were not late again. I always remember those meetings, and even today, I try to not be late for any meeting or appointment.

Planning is crucial to a company's future. But you must also plan to plan.

Preparation will make your planning meeting productive. Know in advance what you want to accomplish. What are your goals? Who will do what? And what is your time line? Think through the items and issues of a planning session. Rehearse the session mentally and visualize how it should come together.

The way you run a meeting or how you participate will have an effect on your career. If you stand out, you will be recognized. If you don't, you will be left in a neutral position and with the rest of the pack.

Worse yet, your lack of meeting skills could portray you as expendable, and that's not what you want.

Remember the best plan can fail if it is not executed properly or on time.

It's amazing how often a company takes the time to plan, spends the money to do it well, and then doesn't get any benefits. The common denominator is usually a lack of top-down attention and tracking, with no one responsible to make it happen.

Many times I've seen plans put together that were in the acceptable to excellent range, and yet they didn't accomplish much of anything. If no one implements the actions recommended or follows up on steps taken, the plan will drift and die.

Whether we are talking about a key meeting or an important planning event, they both involve people and time, the most fundamental elements. If the results can have such a serious effect on your business, why shouldn't the preparation be serious? To make a contribution at your meeting requires time and thought to sift through the issues and information ahead of time. When the stakes are high, the preparation should be even more intense. I have been at too many meetings or planning sessions where people were unprepared, making either no contribution or a poor one that ultimately handicapped the effort.

Decisions are made at meetings. Facts must be available and understood to reach the right one and direct the course of action. Hard work must be done ahead of time to make this possible.

REMEMBER THIS

You must be well prepared before a meeting or planning session. This takes prior effort and hard work. If this doesn't happen, the meeting is unlikely to produce good results. The "pre" part before any meeting or planning can make or break it.

"There is nothing so fatal to character as half-finished tasks."
— David Lloyd George

"One of life's most painful moments comes when we must admit that we didn't do our homework, that we are not prepared."
— Merlin Olsen

"Without involvement, there is no commitment.
Mark it down, asterisk it, circle it, underline it.
No involvement, no commitment."
— Stephen Covey

12. GET INVOLVED IN COMPANY PLANNING

There Is No Substitute for Good Planning

With this chapter, my intent is to recognize that plans are needed to create mile markers for success and must be monitored constantly to see if any adjustments are needed. The detailed process of developing a plan is another subject that many other books explain very well and are worth reading.

To understand planning better, let's reduce it down to the basics. Remember, you are trying to determine how to go from where you are now to another level over a period of time.

- Know what your real position is today.

- Know your strengths, weaknesses, goals, the market you are in, your competition, the forces in your market, and the changes you see coming.

- Where do you want to be in what period of time?

- How do you get there, and why do you want to be there?

- What might be some of the obstacles and opportunities along the way?

Once you have a plan, following it is like driving a car. If you are driving from point A to point B, even on a straight road you must make constant, minor adjustments to the steering wheel or you will go off the road. You cannot just hold the steering wheel firmly in one

position. You must move it, even if only slightly, to stay on course. There are also times when you reach a detour and have to change your route to reach the destination. In other words, when a change needs to be made to succeed, you had better make the change and not follow the original route blindly.

The same is true of following a plan. We all plan even the simplest things, such as what to do each day. Your plan for business or your life requires constant monitoring and adjustments to stay on track. If you follow blindly without looking at the terrain, you will very likely go off track into a possible disaster. We pay far less attention going from point A to B in watching our plans than we do in driving. This is why many plans fail. We develop them but don't monitor them and make needed minor adjustments.

The Eli Broad Graduate School of Management at Michigan State University says in its literature, "Successful companies have a clear strategic focus and a simple way to ensure they are constantly moving toward their ultimate vision. Companies that fail on the other hand, either don't plan or they don't have a systematic formula to produce the results they want. The planning process works best if it is simple. **The reason most companies don't get the results they want is often because they get caught up in the planning and never get to the action part.** By making this process simple, it is easier to create a strategic plan that you can immediately use to get the results." The better you plan, the more likely your business is to succeed.

Even though at this stage in your career you may not be directly involved in formal business planning, you need to understand the principles of planning and use them to be more focused and valuable. Another way to describe this need for planning is to say, "be aware of what is happening in your business." What are the competitive forces, the economic conditions, and the politics? If you know and watch for the vital life signs, you will probably be better equipped to adjust your personal plan and maybe even see that a company is failing before it is obvious to others. Years ago I saw it with the now-defunct Pan Am,

Eastern Air Lines, and now with a few of the current carriers simply by watching their employees on flights and listening to their conversations. As a frequent flyer, I could see the poor attitudes and low execution of fundamentals wherever there was a service to perform.

Bad attitudes, lack of follow-up, failure to respond or to execute a plan or activity—all of these things drag a company and your career to a halt. If there are no goals, no vision, no sense of urgency, no plan, then watch all these fundamental failures follow. They are frustrating to everyone involved, cause other problems, and generate a poor attitude in the company that will eventually cause it to fail. The failures start with management that allows it to happen in the first instance.

Everyone can clearly see the failures of a business: decreased sales, increased customer complaints, employee layoffs, and missed goals. The plan is clearly not working and the actions necessary to fix the plan are not in place or not working.

The corporate plan is the platform, and the airline examples used here illustrates what the customers see when it falls apart.

When I was with ITT, I was transferred to one of its companies, World Communications, in New York City. The division I was assigned to, Data Transmission Systems (DTS), was working on a massive computer project that would allow any fax machine to communicate with any other fax machine, regardless of technology. We had computer programmers writing new software, and we established six large, expensive regional computer centers from coast to coast, all designed to allow the faxes to talk to each other. My role was as a project manager, not as a technician. As I watched the painfully slow progress and the expenses pile up, I thought that our effort might be for nothing. It seemed logical to me that the fax manufacturers would develop technology to allow this cross-communication to take place without us. If this were true, then DTS would be out of business and so might I. When I wondered this aloud to some of our general management, they admitted that they were not confident that DTS did have a long-term life. The more I watched, listened, and read, the more I was convinced this was true. I took this as a sign to look for better long-term possibilities. Within a year, I found a better road to follow, and, as I recall, within the next two years, DTS closed down as technology passed it by.

I offer DTS as an example of a plan that was not properly tracked or monitored. As the years went by, no one wanted to suggest that the original goal of the plan was not likely ever to be reached. No one wanted to take that responsibility, and no one on top forced that kind of decision. Circumstances changed rapidly with newer, faster technology, and the plan was no longer worth pursuing. Don't blindly follow a plan without watching the world around you to see what might influence your goals.

There is no substitute for good fundamental planning that addresses the risks and rewards. I remember when Boston Market, the successful fast-food chain, overexpanded and almost went out of business. I also saw a Burger King franchisee with more than eighty restaurants acquire some other fast-food restaurants and suffer the same overexpansion from growing too fast. Costs were exceeding the revenue stream, and they had to dramatically cut back, risking bankruptcy. In both cases, better planning with the right facts and attention to what could go wrong would have avoided the problems. Don't let prior successes give you unfounded optimism.

Every successful company uses plans to reach the company's goals and monitors and adjusts them regularly.

When you are given the opportunity to get involved in corporate planning, you should take it. If not, ask permission to read a copy of the company plan and study it. You'll not only learn about the company and its goals, but you'll see the format. It's a great learning experience. Once again, you will find yourself in a select minority if you ask to read it.

> ### *REMEMBER THIS*
>
> **Planning is essential and needs to be more than just an exercise. Success requires constant monitoring and adjustments. If circumstances cause a plan to change dramatically, so be it. Don't follow plans blindly if they don't make sense anymore. Get involved in the process and learn what and how your company is planning.**
>
> *"I remember saying to my mentor, 'If I had more money, I would have a better plan.' He quickly responded, 'I would suggest that if you had a better plan, you would have more money.' You see, it's not the amount that counts; it's the plan that counts."*
>
> — Jim Rohn
>
> *"Unless commitment is made, there are only promises and hopes . . . but no plans."*
>
> — Peter Drucker
>
> *"To accomplish great things, we must not only act but also dream, not only plan but also believe."*
>
> — Anatole France

13. NETWORK WITH CONSULTANTS

Be Sure the Goal is Clear

Consultants can play a very productive role in a company's and an individual's success. They can see things that you don't because of their previous experiences with similar circumstances. The consultant's job is to gather the facts and offer recommendations to solve a problem or to make a significant improvement for the company. Even the best consultants would probably concede that they don't know more than their clients, they just have a different experience base. As a client, you must serve as a teacher and a source of information. The consultant can then compare the situation to what he has seen in other cases. Often company management may be too close to the problem to solve it, just as a doctor does not usually treat her own family. The consultant, however, is detached from the company's culture and problems and is more likely to see solutions if he has collected all the facts and properly analyzed them.

If you're looking to hire a consultant, remember these two guidelines:

1.   Don't hire a consulting company unless you have a clearly stated need. Even assuming that the consultants arrive at solid conclusions and recommendations, implementing a program only works if the company and its employees are committed to it.

2.   Always obtain input from the real operations people. One of the difficulties consultants often have is the lack of accurate information and input from throughout the organization. They may be

working at too high a level and not down to the workers where the hands-on experience is. Also, the consultants may include too many junior people, such as recent business school grads who lack the experience to identify the problems and the solutions.

Two examples illustrate these points.

The first was when Pillsbury, Burger King's parent company at that time, sent a well-known consulting company to Burger King, which didn't see the need for the work and didn't support it. Once the consultants completed the job and briefed everyone, the plan was essentially put on the shelf and never implemented. The work the consultants had done was excellent but had not been deemed necessary by Burger King. In addition, Pillsbury never followed up, much less monitored the execution of the plan. **The message here is: don't hire a consulting company unless the client company has a clearly stated need and support of your key people.** If this isn't true, you will have people participating with no intention of implementing the program aggressively.

The second consulting experience happened years later when Pillsbury's (and thus Burger King's) new owner, Grand Metropolitan, a large British company, brought in a reputable Chicago-based consulting company. Grand Metropolitan believed that Burger King needed to reorganize their field operations. The consultants recommended a structure that had been tried eight years earlier and failed. There were only a few executives left in the company who had been there eight years ago, leading to no opposition at that level. However, a larger group of middle managers, who had been there, did remember, but the consultants gave them little chance for input. The reorganization was implemented and failed again for the same reasons as before.

The critical issue was to obtain input from the real operations people. The questions should have been, "Why did this reorganization fail in the past? What were the facts then and now? Can we learn from the past? If the same conditions exist now as they did then, will this prohibit the same type of reorganization again? Can we change the conditions? Should we try?" In this case, the conditions and mind-set of the business were the same, so any new plan had to recognize the seeds for failure in order to create success.

I am reminded of the following insightful quote:

"We trained hard, but it seemed that every time we were beginning to form into teams, we would be reorganized. I was to learn later in life that we tend to meet any new situation by reorganizing, and what a wonderful method it can be for creating the illusion of progress, while producing confusion, inefficiency, and demoralization."

— Petronius Arbiter, 210 BC

If you are fortunate to be selected to work with consultants, watch, listen, and learn. Because the consultants report to a top-level executive in the company, any comments the consultants make about you can reach people at levels you might not normally have an opportunity to meet. If you impress the consultants and build relationships, there is a good chance these connections could advance your career.

REMEMBER THIS

Consultants can be very useful if they resolve a clearly stated need and can obtain the hands-on information from the operations staff. In addition, they make useful contacts for your network because of their knowledge and broad range of contacts.

"The value of an idea lies in the using of it."
— Thomas Edison

"There is nothing as easy as denouncing. It doesn't take much to see that something is wrong, but it does take some eyesight to see what will put it right again."
— Will Rogers

"Unless you try to do something beyond what you have already mastered, you will never grow."
— Ralph Waldo Emerson

---

14. SHARPEN YOUR MANAGEMENT SKILLS

Learn How to Minimize People Problems

In this first section of the book, we've been discussing the professional practices you need to get ahead, and the subject of this chapter, managing, brings them all together. We will be looking at common responsibilities, opportunities, and potential problems that managers deal with all the time.

Your first steps in managing can start from your cubicle before you have any management responsibilities. You can help your boss with ideas and suggestions that may help him to manage better. Sometimes a fresh look can generate a new approach that people have not thought of before. Volunteer to serve on committees and task forces and participate to contribute and to learn. Try to look at situations as a manager would.

Here, I want to offer you key guidelines in managing and must mention that there are many books that delve more deeply into this topic. In particular, I would recommend checking out anything written by Peter Drucker, a world-famous consultant and author.

KEEP UP MORALE

As a manager, you are responsible for the people and the work in your group. Most of a manager's problems and responsibilities are people related—meaning employee relationships, morale, attitude, and performance. A manager must have a productive and happy group of people working as a team. This can be disrupted quickly when there are people problems. They must be solved immediately. All of this can mean success or failure; the stakes are big.

Part of keeping on top of potential issues is regular performance evaluations of your staff. People need honest and constructive critiques of their work in order to improve. You must make time to do them formally and informally.

When people are treated fairly, you will find your job more doable and more enjoyable. Your attitude will directly affect your people. Everything good in your attitude will be reflected by them. This is also true of everything negative.

I can't emphasize enough how essential it is for you as a manager to minimize people problems. You have some control over these problems, but where you don't, you can at least alert your management to them.

When people problems are minimized, you will have more time to do your job, and the company will benefit from increased production at higher quality levels.

When you visit a company, you can tell what the morale and the corporate culture are like. You can see it and hear it. I visit one large company regularly that exudes an atmosphere of tension and basic unfriendly coldness. You can see it in the faces and hear it in the tone of conversations. People who work in offices practically next to each other communicate by e-mail, and workers have very little direct, face-to-face contact with their supervisor. I can only believe the company is paying a high price in low productivity and poor quality of work.

All companies say that people are their most important asset. Some, however, don't really believe it, and the evidence is usually obvious. Fortunately, notable exceptions such as Southwest Airlines, Starbucks, and Johnson & Johnson are known for their people-oriented management style and even have earned high marks from the media for it. When people are treated well and fairly, they become more loyal and take ownership in their work, watching to protect and help their company.

SUPPORT YOUR EMPLOYEES

Without the best people, you will be unlikely to produce the best work. You must bring in the right people, train them, give them what they need to do their job, and support them in every way you can. They will know you are doing these things and will respond positively.

GIVE CREDIT

In that same vein, always give credit to others where it is due and never take credit for something you didn't do. People know when they are being shortchanged. The way to get quality work and creativity from your staff is to give them the recognition they deserve. You win because of their work and because your boss will see you as a good manager for acknowledging them. The company wins because quality work was produced. Nobody loses, and you likely will guarantee that this positive cycle will continue.

People at every level deserve recognition. It's up to you to recognize and reward good performance. I recommend that you read *Managing with Carrots* and *The 24-Carrot Manager,* both by Adrian Gostick and Chester Elton.

DELEGATE

You will accomplish much more when you learn to delegate responsibility to your staff. As we discussed in chapter 5, "Don't Try to Go It Alone," you need other people. Early in my career, I was frequently surprised at how well my people were able to take on new work and often did it better than I could. When you have too much work and you are trying to do too much yourself, you are likely to develop a negative attitude and shortchange some of your responsibilities. Your job is to get the work done on time, correctly, and completely. Delegating allows you time to pursue those responsibilities. It also is a compliment to your staff; they know they are helping you and that they have become more valuable to the company.

REMEMBER THE CUSTOMER

No matter what kind of work you do or what industry you are in, you should always keep a customer's perspective on what you do. Somewhere in the chain there is always a customer, otherwise your company wouldn't be in business. Sometimes the customer is obvious, and other times the customer is several steps removed from what you do. Always remember, the customer is the reason you have your job. Thinking of the customer as you do your job will help you to develop a broad perspective of how everything fits together for your company.

BE APPROACHABLE

Your staff must feel free to see you and bring their ideas and problems to you. Teach them that if there is a work-related problem, they should also bring you a recommended solution. Many in management say they have an "open-door policy," but this overused term has little real meaning. You must demonstrate that you are available to talk to them. The old theory of managing by walking around is still a good policy. Talk to your staff and ask them questions. You'll both learn from this exchange. If your people are afraid to tell you bad news because they know what your reaction will be, they will hide it, or modify the facts—misleading you and causing an even bigger problem. Be careful not to build a wall between you and your people. If there is no true exchange of information top to bottom and bottom to top, everyone will pay the price.

BE KNOWN FOR CHARACTER

To be described as ethical and trustworthy is a powerful testament to your character. The dictionary defines *ethical* as "dealing with morals or principles of morality and pertaining to right and wrong in conduct and also being in accordance with the rules." *Trust* means "reliance on the integrity, strength, ability, and surety of a person or thing." It defines *integrity* as "adherence to moral and ethical principles and soundness to moral character and honesty." I recommend that you read *The Integrity*

Advantage by Adrian Gostick and Dana Telford and *The Bottom Line on Integrity* by Quinn McKay.

Every day we face opportunities to test our integrity. Doing the right thing may not always be easy but does instill confidence in yourself and others.

MEET YOUR OBJECTIVES

As a manager, you have goals to accomplish. Many times these commitments are associated with sales and profits. Or it could also be a program that you and your group must implement. Nothing can hurt you more than not meeting your objective. In the end, this translates to the same thing: you made a commitment and you didn't keep it.

If circumstances are out of your control, create ongoing, open discussions about these factors so that your boss is not surprised by a failure to accomplish a goal. No one wants bad surprises, and the best way to avoid them is to keep the issues in the open for discussion and solutions. Don't hide bad news; deal with it as soon as you know about it. This is why plans can change, and you must keep your finger on the company's pulse to know what is happening and why.

KEEP LEARNING

I doubt there are but a few courses in college that deal with the practical aspects of being a manager. The best way to learn is by watching, asking questions, using common sense, and reading. Watch and ask questions of the best managers you know. Any good manager will be willing to give you advice. Most people will be impressed with a person who asks questions and shows a real interest in the work. Remember that using role models of the best managers that you can watch and know is an excellent way to learn. We will discuss this further in chapter 25, "Choose the Best Role Models." You also must supplement your learning and observation with the experience of actually working with people.

Over the years, I had the good fortune to work for and with many good managers. Although they weren't all the same in terms of personality, work style, goals, and values, they did have some common attributes and characteristics:

- They had a genuine consideration and affection for people.
- They knew the business and had a close knowledge of the customer.
- They had common sense, a clear set of goals and the ability to plan.
- Their staff was loyal and made that extra effort to please their boss.
- They had talent, which became more important the higher they rose in their organizations.

The ones who failed as managers usually had poor people skills, were unreliable, and, more often than not, were self-centered.

I am talking here about managing, which is not the same thing as leading. I knew leaders who were not good managers, and I knew managers who were not true leaders. The definition you've heard before still rings true, "Managers do things right, and leaders do the right thing." Leaders often achieve great breakthroughs, see beyond the norm, and have vision that others don't have.

You will spend your career managing people and can always learn how to improve this skill. When you are given the responsibility to manage, you have the opportunity to make it fulfilling and fun. You will develop relationships that will challenge and enlighten you. Don't be discouraged if you fail occasionally because we all do at one time or another. Remember, bouncing back is an indication of your character and you will be stronger and wiser. This is all part of the experience you will gain over your career. If you are a successful manager, you have the potential to go far.

REMEMBER THIS

Managing is a great opportunity where you will learn, help others, and be helped. A good value system and common sense will serve you well. Watch, ask questions, and rely on those above you and below you; managing is a skill best learned on the job.

"Leadership, like swimming, cannot be learned by reading about it."
— Henry Mintzberg

*"The value of man should be in what he gives
and not what he can receive."*
— Albert Einstein

*"When dealing with people remember you are not dealing with
creatures of logic, but with creatures of emotion."*
— Dale Carnegie

PART TWO

Personal Traits and Practices to Develop

15. HAVE A POSITIVE ATTITUDE

The Personal Trait That Dominates

I'm sure you have heard the word *attitude* used frequently in your company: right attitude, wrong attitude, positive attitude, negative attitude—you've heard it all. It's easy to say "have the right attitude." In my opinion, not enough emphasis is placed on how imperative it is to have the right attitude and how destructive to your company and your career to have the wrong one. **Attitudes are contagious.** An obviously genuine, positive attitude travels from top to bottom quickly, setting the tone of the corporate culture. Just saying "attitude is everything" is meaningless unless reinforced by action.

Think about it, would you rather work with someone pleasant and helpful or someone disagreeable who makes everything difficult?

I have seen people with strong skills and lots of talent fail in their jobs because of poor attitudes. If people don't want to work with you or listen to you, how can you be effective? On the other hand, I have watched people with average talent and a positive attitude succeed because they were well liked and team players.

I stress attitude in this book because you may not understand how much this trait can affect your career.

People do a lot of business because of personal relationships. Unless you have some extraordinary product or service, people would rather deal with a friend who has the same or similar service or product even at a slightly higher price. You must always sell yourself and establish strong relationships.

People like to do business with people they like and trust. Sales reps have always known this, but this is also true in other jobs. Most of us deal with other people all the time. Some are more important to your career than others. Rather than pick and choose, develop friendly, strong relationships with everyone. Remember, it's human nature to want to help and support your friends. In turn, you must be dependable and commit to do what you say. This involves meeting dates, producing reliable information, and even minor tasks such as returning a phone call or e-mail. Make no mistake, there are more failures on this last point than you would expect. When you have to chase someone to return your call, your willingness to do business with that person will begin to erode.

Attitude is a frame of mind that helps you to do things and get them done. This must include being reliable. A positive attitude, not just a big smile and cheery words, has to be associated with progress. To succeed and get it done, you must be dependable and reliable. They all go together. A positive attitude with no accomplishments is shallow.

Over the years, I've noticed that these four areas contribute to positive outlook.

BE COMFORTABLE IN SOCIAL SITUATIONS

Many business situations have social components. You've heard it said that a lot of business is conducted on the golf course. People are more comfortable, and relationships are built in social events that many times have business implications. Some people are very comfortable in connecting the two and just comfortable socially overall.

As a starter, in mixing the two, show an interest in their personal life, family, children, and pets. Remember what their hobbies are, what their children like to do, and trips they have planned. I know a supplier who has a young son who races motorcycles competitively. Whenever I see him, I ask how his son is doing, and my friend's eyes light up. Then I get a full report. Ever since this dialogue started, I have found that all my business dealings have been easier and more profitable, and I also simply enjoy seeing my friend's parental pride.

Try not to be shy when you find yourself in a group of higher-level people, such as at a board meeting dinner or other company event. Ask questions and show interest in others and they will be flattered. If possible, try to learn something about their interests ahead of time. Don't talk about yourself unless you are asked. I remember at a Pillsbury board meeting dinner asking the chairman about running track on his college team because someone had mentioned it to me earlier. This was a good start to a lively conversation.

Nurture your network and invite people to a ball game, dinner, golf, the theater, whatever. Almost everyone enjoys socializing and likes being asked. You can see how relationships build when you can blend business with pleasure. This is easier for some but not everyone. If you are in the latter category, my advice is to relax and treat it as a pure social, fun time and not with the stress you might have in a business situation.

REALLY, REALLY TRY TO BE SINCERE

False interest and flattery are big negatives and easy to detect. You probably have been exposed to this treatment and know the signs. When you see the other person's eyes looking around at other people while asking you about your family, you are not the focus of his attention. This doesn't happen to someone who is sincere. Eyes will tell you quite a lot. As you find out more about someone, you will find that interest in him will often grow.

BE OPTIMISTIC

Always look for the best and avoid dwelling on the negative. However, don't be naive or appear foolish. You must balance the optimism with being realistic. Optimism is contagious and presents a good image.

For example, compare "I really believe we can win this bid, but it depends on how well our field tests succeed" to "I believe the field tests could kill us, and then we'll have no chance to win the bid."

In the first statement, the person is setting a positive tone but with a caution about the importance of the field tests. In the second statement, there is little hope expressed.

BE POLITE

Never be rude, even if you believe you have the right to be. Your position, even if justified and correct, will be lost and only the rudeness will be remembered. This is also true about a cocky attitude. You lose much more than you gain. I have never seen an instance where a positive attitude is not returned by a positive attitude or at least one that promotes cooperation. In addition, be careful about what you say even in jest because you might be misinterpreted or misquoted.

A positive attitude means you are approachable and step forward to help. You listen well and do what you say you will do. You understand the value of supporting, learning, and getting help from others.

REMEMBER THIS

Never underestimate the power of a positive attitude. Learn to be sincere, optimistic, polite, and comfortable in social situations. Combine this with good work and you increase the probability of success.

"There is little difference in people, but that little difference makes a big difference. The little difference is attitude. The big difference is whether it is positive or negative."

— W. Clement Stone

"A professional is a person who can do his best at a time when he doesn't particularly feel like it."

— Alistair Cooke

"This may shock you, but I believe the single most significant decision I can make on a day-to-day basis is my choice of attitude. It is more important than my past, my education, my bankroll, my successes or failures, fame or pain, what other people think of me or say about me, my circumstances, or my position. Attitude is that 'single string' that keeps me going or cripples my progress. It alone fuels my fire or assaults my hope. When my attitudes are right, there's no barrier too high, no valley too deep, no dream too extreme, no challenge too great for me."

— Charles R. Swindoll

16. BE RESPONSIVE AND RELIABLE

Two of the Most Basic Essentials

How frustrated are you when someone does not respond to your message? How many times do you have to ask for the same thing because you received no response the first few times you asked? How do you feel about those people who don't get back to you?

You probably have a clear image of what I mean and also a poor opinion of people like that.

Knowing this, you don't want to be branded the same way. You would much rather be known as a reliable person who responds promptly.

I work with a key person in an associated company who is extremely knowledgeable, very likeable, and possesses a good sense of humor. However, he doesn't reply to your messages and requires a lot of follow-up. Not surprisingly, he has earned a reputation for being unreliable. If he says, "I'll send you a copy," chances are he will not. Although people seem to accept this for now, it's only a matter of time before his reputation seriously damages his career. I know how much more valuable he could be if he took the time to be better organized and responsive.

You have no idea of the price you pay for not being dependable. For example, an associate was looking for a talented, reliable assistant to fill an important job in a division recently formed in the company. She reduced the search to two people of almost equal ability, though one was considered to be more reliable than the other. Actually, the less reliable candidate may have even been a bit more talented, but the question of reliability made the choice easy for my friend. This kind of decision happens all the time.

In another example, a colleague had received a phone message and didn't respond for a few days because the name of the caller and the company were unfamiliar to her. Later, she discovered that the caller was doing basic due diligence for a major buyer that had singled out her company. The consequence was the loss of a $2 million order because the caller reported back to his buyer that the supplier was not responsive.

Lack of follow-up could also mean a colleague who never gets comments back to you on a report you sent him. If you are keeping track, you'll probably have to chase it down. What is your opinion of the person who never responds to you? Once or even twice may be acceptable, but a pattern makes that person unreliable. If the lack of response causes some loss or damage to your company, then the consequences are even more serious.

Unresponsiveness may pervade a company's or department's culture, as in the following case. A major credit card company's customer service department had a serious problem around addressing letters about disputed charges. Department members wouldn't contact the customer until they had an answer; meanwhile, the customer didn't know what was going on with the complaint. A new executive was brought in and implemented a system where the customer received a call within twenty-four hours or less upon receipt of the letter—a simple acknowledgment that the department was looking into the complaint.

Although the response didn't resolve the actual complaint, it did reassure the customer that an answer was forthcoming—and reduced the complaints about customer service. Along those same lines, if someone is waiting for an answer from you, let her know you are working on it. Checking in is part of reliability. Never leave someone in limbo.

If you have trouble responding, you may not be as well organized as you should be. Take the time to learn about time management or you will hurt your career. The effect on your reputation is very difficult to recoup once the damage is done.

Not responding also conveys "no sense of urgency." When you look for people to promote, you expect them to have their priorities and those of the company in order.

Another damaging form of unresponsiveness is procrastination, such as not returning telephone calls or returning them too late to be effective. You never win by delaying what has to be done. There could be times when something you were supposed to do has seemingly been forgotten, or you could get lucky and your assignment may be determined unnecessary. But remember, someone important may know you didn't complete your assignment. A company with high standards isn't going to accept procrastination.

I can tell you that these poor business habits can destroy your reputation and credibility and damage opportunities for your business. I don't believe anyone can effectively remember all the actions that require attention, but I rarely see people take notes to do something.

So then, how do you remedy these poor traits? It's simple. Keep an ongoing "To Do" list on a special pad where you always jot down what you have to do. You can also use a three-ringed appointment book with pages for your list or a PDA to note priorities. As an item is completed, just cross it out. Always carry a pad with you—perhaps a small one that fits in your coat, shirt pocket, or briefcase. Use this and then transfer it to your master "To Do" list. It's that easy. You'll never forget to do what needs to be done and gain a reputation for being reliable and organized.

These lists can help reduce a sense of being overwhelmed that can create procrastination because you will clearly see what's on your plate. Procrastination also is often about fear of making a mistake or not being engaged in the task. The energy spent worrying about and avoiding the task could be better channeled on the work. Start with the easiest part first and soon you'll be moving along.

Being unreliable is a sure sentence to failure. The degree of failure can range from being unpromotable to being fired.

One last comment on reliability, we all have to make guesses and estimates from time to time, such as with forecasts or project timelines. There is a tendency to exaggerate and offer the most optimistic estimate rather than a realistic one. You may promise something in three days when you know it is more is likely to take seven to ten. Perhaps you predict sales at a certain level by the end of the first quarter when the second quarter is more realistic. This habit of repeatedly making off-target promises will also label you as unreliable. Your reputation and credibility are at stake. There's a business saying: "Under-promise and over-deliver." I would change that maxim to "Keep your promises and over-deliver."

Finally, remember that being reliable and responsive is not a *sometimes* thing. It's an *always* thing. That's what reliable means. **When you hear someone described as "steady as a rock" or "old reliable," they are not referring to an average performer.**

REMEMBER THIS

There is no substitute for being responsive. It builds on your reputation for being reliable and can only help your career. Being reliable and responsive are two of the very basic traits you should be known for. They require discipline and attention to organization. The consequences of not having them will limit your career.

"Continuous effort, not strength or intelligence, is the key to unlocking our potential."
— Winston Churchill

"The kind of people I look for to fill top management spots are the eager beavers, the mavericks. These are the people who try to do more than they're expected to do—they always reach."
— Lee Iacocca

"Ninety percent of success is just showing up."
— Woody Allen

17. BE A DOER, NOT JUST A TALKER

Step Forward and Volunteer

This is about promises and results. Many people promise but don't produce. Unfortunately, this can be more the norm than the exception.

Because many people don't extend themselves to help beyond their normal job responsibilities, you should take the initiative, be creative, and find a better way. Remember, though: once you volunteer, you must deliver.

In my first year at the New Jersey Bell Telephone Company, my first job after college and a tour of duty in the U.S. Air Force, I designed a new worksheet to make my job easier doing traffic-engineering calculations. I showed it to my supervisor who made it a standard form for our department. As simple as that was, my initiative demonstrated creativity and that, in a short time, helped me to get my first promotion.

A few years later, I served as the information systems manager with ITT's Puerto Rico Telephone Company in San Juan. I developed a program to compute calculations for work that everyone was doing manually on a regular basis. I drew up a flow chart and had one of the computer programmers code it. This earned me an unscheduled bonus from the president of the company because he viewed the program as innovative and creative.

These are two simple cases of recognizing an opportunity and taking the initiative to act. When you do this, you are likely to be noticed and set yourself apart from the others. **The executives who decide your future look for doers and volunteers who commit and produce. These executives are not likely to confuse activity with progress.**

If you were a supervisor, wouldn't you want people in your group who could be counted on to step forward and do the job on time? As fundamental as this is, there are not enough who match this profile. When you do, it becomes one more advantage for you.

I'll never forget one of the most impressive examples of actions speaking louder than words. When now-Senator Bob Graham was the governor of Florida, he initiated a tradition of spending several days per year as "work days" in different jobs to experience each firsthand.

One day during my time at Burger King, I received a call from his office asking if he could schedule a day to work in a Burger King restaurant. Of course, we were eager to make arrangements to schedule the governor at a Burger King convenient for him, but his office said the restaurant could be our choice.

We set it up for Fort Lauderdale at one of our better restaurants and didn't issue any prior media releases. Graham wanted the true experience without the crowd that might have been drawn with publicity. I met him and two of his staffers at 8:00 a.m. He was very friendly and asked to be briefed about his duties. He started around 8:30 a.m. working behind the counter in uniform along with the regular employees. Graham worked almost the whole day. We had lunch together, burgers, of course, and he asked about employee benefits, duties, average length of stay, and other general questions about the restaurant and staff.

Besides his obvious commitment to doing this regularly, I learned that he was seeking to know something about the vital life signs of each industry. Graham wanted to know what was important to the employees and to the company. The PR he gained from these work days was not the major reason for this routine. His real gain was insight that would help him in his job.

In business there are times when you must take the lead and have a choice of action or words. You must decide what is needed, and if it is action, you must take it. This can be as easy as deciding whether or not to visit a branch office. If the action of visiting is what is needed, then words alone are not enough. You may hear a colleague say that he is an idea man and not an operations type. **The reality is most of us have ideas from time to time, but those who turn words into actions are the ones who move ahead.**

REMEMBER THIS

Step forward, volunteer, commit, and then do it. Many people talk and promise, but few actually deliver. If you do, you will stand out from the crowd.

"Effective leaders are not preachers, they are doers."
— Peter Drucker

"Actions can say more than words,
but without words actions can be meaningless."
— Michael McEwan

"Well done is better than well said."
— Benjamin Franklin

---

18. ANTICIPATE AND ADAPT TO CHANGE

Transform Yourself

Change is inevitable.

This is especially true in our world today due to technology and all the benefits that technology produces, which includes increased capacity and speed so that the rate of change is faster than ever. Faster computers, more memory, faster communications—and all of this at lower costs drives change, and you must be ready to act.

Change today comes quickly and only those who look and plan for it will benefit.

Be alert, learn, and ask questions. Talk to others who you respect. Read the newspaper (especially the business section), key publications, and watch the many good TV news programs and documentaries.

The key is to react quickly and appropriately, taking care not to overreact or underreact. Ignoring the changes and assuming they will go away or that their effects will be small is not a wise path to follow.

Here are three basic steps to keep in mind:

1. **WATCH FOR COMING CHANGE.** What changes do you see ahead that might affect you and your job? They may not be easy to recognize but careful, diligent observation will teach you. Dig deep, ask questions, and listen. Talk to your boss and check in with your network.

In chapter 8, "Ask for What you Want," I cited an example of inquiring about changes you see. I referred to an ITT company called Data Transmission Systems (DTS). If you recall, a technical group of programmers and computer operations people were developing a way to translate fax languages so that any fax machine could communicate with any other. This elaborate network of programs would use major computer centers from coast to coast switching fax messages to different types of fax machines all over the country.

If you recall, my reaction after I had been there a few months was that we might be behind the curve and that the fax manufacturers would solve the communication problem without our switching centers. Because of this concern about DTS's future, I took the chief planning officer position at Burger King Corporation, giving up fifteen years at ITT. A couple of years later, DTS Systems was closed.

2. **RECOGNIZE THE FIRST SIGNS OF CHANGE**, whether gradual or sudden. Gradual change can be easier to manage because you are probably watching the events unfold on a regular basis. Sudden change is more dangerous because you don't see it coming.

In the case of the dot-coms, I would say the bust happened gradually, but you still could have anticipated problems. Their poor financial performance was a key, and the investors were becoming anxious. Should they continue to pour capital into their investment to protect it or stop?

Evolving over the years, the computer revolution has affected people and businesses in many different ways. Businesses that have not kept pace with the new technology may jeopardize their future by not having a strong electronic infrastructure. You can't count on catching up. In a similar vein, people in the workforce who resist using computers and understanding computer programs are making themselves vulnerable and may not be able to survive change.

Usually the signs of change can be seen, and the experts in the financial and operational worlds are looking closer than you are. That's why you must read, observe, ask questions, and use common sense to recognize what is happening. Then, you can take protective actions and draw up a back-up plan, especially for your career.

3. HAVE A PLAN FOR YOURSELF AND YOUR COMPANY. Map out in advance how you and your company can benefit, or if you can't, what you should do. Without overreacting, develop several "what if" scenarios and see how you could be affected. If you had been a dot-commer, for example, you might have seen your stock value dropping. Then you might have realized the main reason for being with your company was the value of the stock options. Finally, recognizing that your company wasn't going to change direction, you could conclude that you should begin your job search.

Be alert and check the options. In times of change, can you play a role to help your company? How do you see your role affected by these changes? Knowing all this, you are empowered to decide what your future will be. Change will never stop and will come quicker now because of faster communications, the speed of technology, and the overall ability to make things happen faster. Change often generates fear, but realize that resistance is not an option. Change can offer fresh opportunities leading to new products, new ways to work, and new careers. Change is really transformation.

REMEMBER THIS

Change is a fact of work life. You should not ignore change but deal with it every day. Watch for change, recognize it and its effect on your job, and develop plans for how to deal with it in your company and your career.

"It is not necessary to change. Survival is not mandatory."
— W. Edwards Deming

"Change before you have to."
— Jack Welch

"Progress is impossible without change,
and those who cannot change their minds cannot change anything."
— George Bernard Shaw

19. BE OPEN AND FRIENDLY

Honey Gets Better Results Than Vinegar

One of my favorite sayings is "You catch more flies with honey than vinegar." We all are more cooperative and friendly when we are treated politely and pleasantly. I've watched executives who were so affable and magnetic that, without using threats and demands, they could get their staff to perform at the highest level. Simply stated, you are looking for results in one way or another, and you are more likely to get them using honey.

I'll always remember in my early days at the New Jersey Bell Telephone Company, when I was a trainee right out of college and the U.S. Air Force. I was talking with an associate. We were joined by Len Bishop, a division manager, a remarkable level of success, even if you achieved no more in your career. I was impressed, even in awe that a man at his level would stop to speak with us. A Southern gentleman, he was friendly and genuinely interested in our conversation. He understood the value of honey versus vinegar. I met him only one other time, and yet I still remember him so clearly.

You also know that if you are angry and unfriendly you are likely to be treated the same way or with a cold, reserved attitude. If anger is countered with friendliness and a helpful attitude, it is almost always diffused.

Maybe the key ingredient in maintaining your cool is patience. A professional, friendly, calm approach to problems and unmet requests is usually most effective. No one likes to deal with impatient, contentious, and inflexible people. Often putting yourself in the other peoples' positions can help you better understand their situations and get the results you are seeking.

Think over your experiences where you have either been disagreeable or had to deal with someone who was. What were the results? Now think of situations where the attitudes were positive. What were the results?

You can and should expect people to meet commitments and schedules. When they don't, find out why not but don't jump to conclusions. Get the facts and then decide on a solution. First, you need to get what you originally wanted, say, a report or a delivery. Then determine how the delay can be avoided in the future. Someone may be at fault, but maybe the circumstances were out of his or her control. Learn which it is and then act reasonably.

One reason to always respond with honey instead of vinegar is because you don't want to "burn your bridges," another favorite saying. What follows is a true story that demonstrates the wisdom of both sayings.

A large European manufacturer had appointed one of their fast-track superstars to run its American subsidiary. Bilingual and people-oriented, he was a skilled leader and manager well positioned to be a future leader of the parent company. Although he was not seeking opportunities with other companies, he was frequently contacted by headhunters. One day he received an offer he could not refuse, to be president of a company larger than his own parent company located in his own country. The salary was about four times larger than his, and yet, despite all this he still paused to consider the move because of his strong loyalties to his present company.

He finally decided to visit the chairman of his parent company and tell him of the situation. He said that an opportunity like this is not likely to come again, and he didn't see how he could achieve a position like this in the parent company. (I must mention that the company offering him the position had the potential to be a large customer of his present company.) If he joined the new company, he would likely become a big customer. Unfortunately, the chairman of his parent company became angry and asked him to clean out his desk and leave that day.

The chairman should have realized that this new job was too good to refuse and turned this unhappy situation into opportunity of gaining a new big customer. After all, the employee was going to be leaving anyway, so why not keep the relationship, wish him every success, and secure a new customer? That's exactly the approach McKinsey & Company takes.

This well-known global consulting firm has enjoyed great success when their consultants leave to join the companies they were originally sent to help. McKinsey realized these people would be great sales persons for them and likely bring McKinsey back to do regular consulting. Therefore, they wished the departing employees the best of luck and cemented new relationships.

The moral of the story is that "honey works, not vinegar" when you are faced with a situation of a key person departing for another job. You are going to lose the person anyway, so why not make a customer instead of an enemy.

Remember that burning bridges is usually applied to the employee leaving, but not in the story I just told. It works both ways.

Needless to say, your departure isn't the time to vent your anger and frustration but rather to be professional with constructive advice about how you see things and some good recommendations. This extends to conversations with others in the company and outside of it who might report your anger and frustration back to the company. You never know if you could be recruited for a bigger job at that same company, or a future employer might call your former company for a reference. This is real, and it happens.

You always win when you are accessible, friendly, and cooperative. People know in advance how they will be treated and look forward to communicating with you. This doesn't mean you can't be firm, decisive, and focused, but you must learn how to uncover facts, reach conclusions, and get things done with open, friendly behavior. You lose if you are negative, inflexible, and difficult. This is true no matter how much knowledge and talent you have. Why put yourself and your career at a disadvantage when you don't have to?

Once you build a wall that keeps people away or makes them feel uneasy to see you, the chances of achieving success are limited—even if you are a senior executive who has power by virtue of your title.

As you are starting to build your career, your image and reputation are part of the foundation for your path to success. All the good executives that I knew over the years, with few exceptions, had these qualities of accessibility, friendliness, and cooperation.

REMEMBER THIS

You are looking for results in one way or another. You are always more likely to get them using honey—open, friendly behavior—than vinegar—anger and fear. The results you get from vinegar may produce some immediate success, but the long-lasting effects will produce a lingering bad taste with many people you are going to need along the way.

"It was one of the rules which, above all others, made Benjamin Franklin the most amiable of men in society: never to contradict anybody."

— Thomas Jefferson

"Am I not destroying my enemies when I make them my friends?"

— Abraham Lincoln

"Consider how much more you often suffer from your anger and grief than from those things for which you are angry or grieved."

— Marcus Aurelius

20.PUT IN EXTRA TIME AND EFFORT

The Road to Success Is Open 24/7

Inever met anyone successful who didn't put in the effort and extra hours. Success calls for taking work home and spending some time away from the office thinking about the job.

Achieving success in business isn't easy for most of us and takes more effort than many are willing to expend. You need to work harder, learn more, and spend the time thinking about your job and ways to make a bigger contribution.

Why is this true? Certainly, the number of hours isn't the gauge for success; it's the interest and dedication needed to excel. In the rarest exceptions is it possible to finish at 5:00 p.m., shut everything out of your mind until 9:00 a.m. the next day, and be on top of your job. You need to love what you do, or at least like it a lot. This is the common characteristic found in winners and a major part of the success formula.

The following is extracted from an article by the late Mark H. McCormack, chairman of the Cleveland-based IMG, as written in his monthly newsletter, *Success Secrets*.

"I always get a little confused when I hear people complain about how much work they have on their plates.

I'm not talking about people who are actually bragging when they complain about their workloads, who wear the burdens of their jobs like a badge of honor, a symbol of their indispensability, of how much other folks need and rely on them.

Rather, I'm focusing on people who are genuinely annoyed by the demands of their jobs.

The complaints confuse me because I can't see how otherwise intelligent people overlook one of the most obvious paradoxes in the workplace.

When it comes to duties of the job, the goal is more work, not less. The most successful people in business—from assistant to CEO—never have a perfectly proportioned workload that somehow is cleared up at the end of each eight-hour day.

On the contrary, the most successful people at any company seem to have more work than they can handle.

And that's the way they want it. They appreciate the 'more work, not less' paradox. They understand that the condition of being slightly overwhelmed on the job comes with significant career perks.

For one thing, it increases your exposure—to colleagues, ideas, projects, opportunities, mentors, future bosses, future allies. That only makes sense. The more you have to do, the more you have to throw yourself into the mix of the workplace. That's how you learn and get better.

This improvement generally doesn't go unnoticed. When people see that you can get things done, they more readily gravitate toward you when they want something done. This invariably means more work rather than less."

Along those same lines, the late Harold Geneen, former CEO and chairman of ITT, had a theory about the executive with a cluttered desk. "Show me a manager who has no papers on his desk and I'll show you a manager who isn't managing," said Geneen. In the same way, I say show me a manager who doesn't take some work home at least some nights, and I'll show you a manager who probably doesn't spend the time needed to be successful.

Some sacrifice is needed to achieve. For most of us, this translates into time. Whether it is actually doing work, such as writing a report, reading, or just thinking and planning, success takes time.

In the normal course of a day, there are interruptions, unplanned meetings, and problems that all take time away. This means you probably can't finish all the work you planned to do. You can put it off for tomorrow or do the really important stuff after 5 p.m. It's your choice. Anyone who has achieved some level of success admits it required more effort than most were willing to give.

My ITT days are excellent examples of long days and extra hours. I can remember the extra effort that was essential in every ITT company I worked for in my fifteen years there. If you were a manager and if you wanted to move up, you had to put in the time to make your mark. This dedication was needed to stay ahead or just even with your workload and to meet the requirements of your job.

Frankly, I found that the extra effort gave me more job satisfaction and increased what I could contribute. My bosses recognized my dedication, and I know it played a role in promotions and salary increases.

In short, you will get what you give.

REMEMBER THIS

Achieving success takes more time than an eight-hour day allows. You must sacrifice some of your free time and put in the extra effort, but if you love your job, you won't consider it a sacrifice.

"Unless you are willing to drench yourself in your work
beyond the capacity of the average person, you are
just not cut out for positions at the top."

— J. C. Penney

"I learned that the only way you are going to get anywhere in life
is to work hard at it. Whether you are a musician, a writer,
an athlete, or a businessman, there is no getting around it.
If you do, you'll win—if you don't, you won't."

— Bruce Jenner

"The starting point of all achievement is desire.
Keep this in mind. Weak desires bring weak results,
just as a small fire makes a small amount of heat."

— Napoleon Hill

---

21. HELP PEOPLE

Including Your Boss

I'm sure that somewhere along the way in your career someone helped you in a significant way. This is probably true even if it is early in your career. Helping out is human nature, and the benefits are often intangible, like feeling better about yourself.

There are three rewards for helping others.

1. When you help someone, you gain mastery over a subject ,just as a teacher does.

2. You may very well be helping someone who will succeed and be able to help you later. High-level executives often reach back into their past to bring on board associates who supported them earlier in their career.

3. When you help someone, they are not likely to forget, and you are likely to always remember your good deed. It's good for the soul.

Don't limit yourself to helping only associates. Look for every opportunity to help your boss. The obvious benefits are very clear.

First, you might get your boss promoted, and you may very well advance with her.

Second, your help won't go unnoticed by your boss and her superiors. Their attention can help boost your career. This is a win-win-win situation for you, your boss, and the company.

Ignoring an opportunity to help your boss results in two negatives. First, your lack of support could be obvious to your boss. He may see you as someone who puts yourself first in a selfish effort to succeed. Even if he doesn't, you may be seen as incapable of helping out.

Second, if your boss fails, you may be seen as one of those factors that caused the failure. Then, your boss could be replaced with someone not supportive of you.

I have seen the drawbacks when someone doesn't support his supervisor. I reported to a young executive who rose rapidly to become the chairman and CEO of a major company. I enjoyed watching him use his planning and communication skills. A leader who showed great potential, he was rewarded for his accomplishments by being promoted to head up a major group at the parent company. I soon noticed he wasn't providing complete support for his boss. Instead of creating an atmosphere of cooperation, he became an adversary. The result was that his boss, who needed help, eventually failed, and my friend also failed. Sadly, his career declined rapidly. He never did get it back on track. If he had lent the support his boss needed, maybe they both would have succeeded.

How do you help your boss to get promoted? You need to know where your boss needs help. Logically, you could merely ask him. Develop a relationship so that your boss will tell you and even confide in you. You should also try to produce only your best work, with all of your recommendations based on solid facts. Sloppy, incomplete work will always reflect badly on you and could hurt your boss. If he should send your work forward and it is discredited, then you will lose along with your boss.

Never go to your boss without some recommendations, and ensure that your work contains conclusions and solutions. Always think through your work thoroughly to anticipate questions. Use the "Ask Why" theory from chapter 3, "Tackle Problems

Head-On," where each recommendation must pass the "Why" question at least three to five times. He may not agree with your recommendation, but if the facts and options are presented clearly, then you both have a chance to discuss them and come to a conclusion.

When you are helping or being helped at any level in the organization, don't forget to always give credit where it is due. When credit should be shared for work well done, be sure you make the proper acknowledgements.

These gestures of recognition will pay you back as people will always give their best efforts and performance when they know they'll be properly credited.

When you help an associate or your boss, you all win. Above all, when you help others, you help yourself by displaying the best parts of yourself.

REMEMBER THIS

Help others just as people help you. You can't lose and have much to gain. You learn when you help and the one supported will remember. Helping your boss has multiple benefits and could increase your success along with the boss's. If you don't help an associate or your boss, expect negative consequences.

"Be an opener of doors for such as come after thee,
and do not try to make the universe a blind alley."
— Ralph Waldo Emerson

"There is no doubt about it, appreciation in any form at any time
brightens anyone's existence. And, like a beam of sunlight striking a
mirror, the brightness is reflected back to you."
— Unknown

"For what we get, we can make a living;
what we give, however, makes a life."
— Arthur Ashe

22. HAVE A CARING HEART

What Goes Around Comes Around

Never forget that the people who surround you at work and in life have feelings and needs, just as you do. They also often play a role in your success or failure. As a matter of fact, you have to count on many of them daily. Doesn't it make sense, then, that you should demonstrate a real interest in them? Show them that you care, that their needs and problems are not ignored by you. Knowing something about each of them helps. This personal touch will pay dividends and probably add something to their support for you. Connections with colleagues can only increase your overall enjoyment of your job.

In my experience I've known executives who did care but were afraid to show any real feelings or interest in others. Their demeanor and actions didn't encourage open dialogue with their people. Consequently, a wall was built, stopping the flow of information needed to manage.

The best bosses I had in every one of my jobs over the years always displayed a true interest in others. I responded by doing all that I could to perform well for them. I still remember all those people, going back more than forty years. I often wish that I could see them again to thank them for their support.

In chapter 26, "Review Your Career," I list the names of each one who influenced me in my career and encourage you to do so. I can say that, without exception, all the winners, all the ones who achieved success and who influenced my career and life, had big hearts.

Here are two points that can make a difference:

First, you can't fake a caring attitude. People can read your eyes and body language. They intuitively know the signs when you don't care or aren't listening. Remember, your eyes tell it all, so don't be looking around; instead, focus on the person.

Second, you must really listen to that person. This means paying full and undivided attention while the person is telling you something. You shouldn't be thinking of what you are going to say next. Your attention displays your interest in what they are talking about.

A while back I received an e-mail from a friend, Joe Nelson, that cleverly illustrates the subject of caring. The author is unknown.

Take this short quiz—it will make you think!

• *Name the five wealthiest people in the world.*

• *Name the last five Heisman trophy winners.*

• *Name the last three winners of* American Idol.

• *Name ten people who have won the Nobel or Pulitzer Prize.*

• *Name the last half dozen Academy Award winners for best actor and actress.*

• *Name the last decade's worth of World Series winners.*

How did you do? The point is, none of us remember the headliners of yesterday.

These are no second-raters. They are the best in their fields. But the applause dies. Awards tarnish. Achievements are forgotten. Accolades and certificates are forgotten and buried with their owners.

So, here's another quiz. See how you do on this one.

• *List a few teachers who aided your journey through school.*

• *Name three friends who have helped you through a difficult time.*

• *Name five people who have taught you something worthwhile.*

• *Think of a few people who have made you feel appreciated and special.*

• *Think of five people you enjoy spending time with.*

• *Name half a dozen heroes whose stories have inspired you.*

Easier?

The lesson? The people who make a difference in your life are not the ones with the most credentials, the most money, or the most awards. They are the ones who care.

REMEMBER THIS

In the course of doing business, you work with many people. You help them, and they help and support you. Doing this on an impersonal basis is a disadvantage to both of you. A close, caring bond is not only more productive, but the teamwork and a family environment created help all the players.

"You cannot do a kindness too soon,
for you never know how soon it will be too late.
— Ralph Waldo Emerson

"Everyone wants to be appreciated, so if you appreciate someone,
don't keep it a secret."
— Mary Kay Ash

"If you find it in your heart to care for somebody else,
you will have succeeded."
— Maya Angelou

---

23. BE GRACIOUS AT WINNING AND LOSING

No One Likes a Bragger or a Whiner

When you experience those times in your career when you are promoted or achieve a significant victory, such as a big sale, you will feel elated. People will congratulate you, and you'll gain a lot of attention. This is the time to be a bit humble. Some will be jealous of your achievement. Others will be truly happy for you, and the rest won't much care. Therefore, it's in your best interest to control your emotions and thank your well-wishers, being as gracious and sincere as you can be.

This may all seem obvious to you, but I have seen people's personalities change right before my eyes. I remember on more than a few occasions seeing people break their relationships with the people who had been their peers. They didn't realize that the promotion was just a first step, and they would still need the support, talents, and cooperation from their associates. Remember, you can't do it alone. You must have the best people helping you.

I can say that in almost every case where the person graciously shows acceptance while maintaining a sense of humor and a positive attitude, the future is much brighter. People will respect you, and in the long run, your behavior will favorably affect your career.

On the other side of the coin are the situations where you come out on the losing side. The scrutiny could be rather intense. People will be overly curious to see how you react. You might find yourself in this position if you don't get a promotion or are demoted when someone is placed over you in a newly created job. Along the way, this happens to many of us. **It is a sign of your character, strength, and perseverance to rebound and get back on track.**

You will, and must, bounce back. Remember most people hit the valley in their career or their life. Success, depending on how you define it, doesn't come to everyone all the time, but failure will visit you in one way or another. A classic example was when the legendary Lee Iacocca was fired by Ford Motor Company; he bounced back into the top position at Chrysler and established his legacy. Losing your job at the highest level, as he did, is not likely to present financial problems, but the failure certainly attacks the ego. More recently, Mel Karmazin, former CEO of media giant Viacom, resigned and quickly rebounded to become CEO of the cutting-edge corporation Sirius Satellite Radio.

When you hit a low point, try to learn from the experience. Don't drop out socially or out of your network. The better you handle your problem, the more likely someone will be to give you another opportunity down the road. When this happens, you must try even harder to rebuild your career and reputation.

I remember a former associate, a vice president in a key financial position at Burger King Corporation, who was demoted to a lesser title in the same job. At the time, Burger King was trying to reduce the number of vice presidents rather arbitrarily to fit parameters established by a task force. This person was extremely competent and well respected.

Over the years, every officer in that company, some thirty-five, left for one reason or another, while this solid, reliable performer is still there doing the same fine work he always has done. He was never elevated to his former title but has built a very happy life for himself and his family. He will retire soon as a financially secure young man and will probably enjoy doing some consulting. He took the demotion for what it was worth, shedding some stress along the way, and created a new definition for success for himself.

I also remember a young junior executive named Charlie Hugel at the New Jersey Bell Telephone Company who was clearly tagged to be a star. As I watched him rise within the company, I noticed that he never lost touch with his former peers. They would still go to lunch regularly and even attend social events together. Charlie never lost his common touch and identification with his roots. He later went on to several top executive positions and ended up as chairman at The R. J. Reynolds Company, and the *good guy* in the bestselling book *Barbarians At The Gates* (HarperBusiness), by Bryan Burrough and John Heylar. Charlie never seemed to be affected by his outstanding achievements and was a gracious winner.

REMEMBER THIS

Be prepared for both victories and defeats. Handle each with dignity and continue to be gracious to all your associates. Show yourself to be a winner, no matter what the circumstances are.

"You are not finished if you lose.
You are not finished until you quit."
— Calvary Church, Grand Rapids, Michigan

"The only time you can't afford to fail is the last time you try."
— Charles Kettering

"You may have to fight a battle more than once to win it."
— Margaret Thatcher

---

24. LEARN TO ENJOY YOUR WORK

If You Can't, Look Elsewhere; Don't Retire on the Job

Other than being out of a job, just "putting in time" is one of the worst ways to spend one's professional life. Measuring your day until 5:00 p.m. or counting the days until the weekend, your next vacation, or even retirement is a sure sign you don't like your job.

Don't waste your life living like this. Every day should count and not be wasted. One of the great joys of life is doing work you love.

A simple way to help you enjoy your work more is to always be upbeat and positive. Smiles and friendly behavior will bring you the same in return. Workplace surveys consistently demonstrate that the pleasant workplace plays a significant role in overall job satisfaction. It's in this environment that you do your best work and get more fulfillment from what you do.

Good waiters and waitresses learned this a long time ago. Did you ever notice in a restaurant that when your server was friendly, happy, and helpful you remembered that and were more tolerant of an average meal. On the other hand, a disagreeable server can overshadow excellent food.

Being engaged in your work can also increase your job satisfaction. Try to learn how to do your job better and be a problem solver. Your efforts will hopefully be recognized and rewarded. If they are not, stay positive and be persistent. Find out why your efforts go unrewarded.

Are your efforts really that good? Talk to your boss and be candid. Your boss will more than likely try to be constructive and helpful. This discussion could help in one way or another. You will either learn what you need to do to perform better, or your boss will pay more attention to your contributions and help coach you.

This discussion with your boss is, at minimum, a good step towards establishing or strengthening a relationship that will benefit both of you and help you enjoy your work. Your boss doesn't want to work in isolation. She needs communication on a regular basis as much as you do. Don't retreat into a withdrawn, noncommunicative, unhappy mind-set. You will find that relationships make your job more fun and productive. You will learn more, care more, and make more progress.

Job satisfaction also comes when you know you are making a contribution, know what you are doing, and know you are of real value to your company. Of course, it helps if you feel you are being fairly compensated. What I find interesting, though, is that the job satisfaction and recognition for outstanding work are often more important than the compensation. If you are fairly, or even generously, compensated for your efforts but have real doubts about your value to the company, you will find you are not comfortable with your situation. This doubt creates insecurity. I know this from watching people in those instances. The answer is to make sure your true value increases, and you know your contribution is valued.

To enjoy your work, there are several factors that play a part. In every one of them, you must take the initiative to make things better, and this includes how you build relationships and seek support. Once again, a positive attitude is the basis for all the good things that can come to you in your job.

Body language also broadcasts your attitude to others. This quick self-analysis can tell you what other people could be seeing in you. If you walk lazily as you go from one task, meeting, or event to another, you appear to have no sense of urgency and don't care what comes next. If you walk with your head hanging down, you look like a defeated, unmotivated person. Make an effort to walk with your head up and with a pleasant expression on your face. Interestingly, current research shows that the act of smiling (even faking a smile) can release brain chemicals that promote positive feelings.

If after all of this you still don't like your job, then it's time to see if you can be transferred to another department or group. Look at all of your options and your strengths to see what could be the right solution. What would the ideal or an acceptable job look like? I realize that many people focus on job security, which is certainly important. However, you are opening the door to other options that may afford more enjoyment and security than your current situation. Give everything an honest and objective analysis.

The key is this: to be successful in your career and to enjoy life, you should like your work. I have enjoyed most of my jobs and have felt a sense of accomplishment in each of them. I believe my children, though, have succeeded far beyond me in being in jobs they love to do. The four of them have careers in such varied fields as academia, microbiology research, jewelry making, and a start-up agency placing technology workers. They all measure success by their love for their work and a sense of real accomplishment in serving other people.

REMEMBER THIS

If you don't enjoy your work and your job, it is unlikely that you will succeed. You must take the initiative to make it better. Communication and a positive attitude are the two tools to make it happen.

"As you walk down the fairway of life you must smell the roses, for you only get to play one round."

— Ben Hogan

"To love what you do and feel that it matters —how could anything be more fun?"

— Katherine Graham

"If you are too busy to enjoy life, you are too busy."

— Jeff Davidson

---

25. CHOOSE THE BEST ROLE MODELS

Learn from People Who Know More Than You Do

Remember when you were a kid and would try to emulate the heroes you'd see at the movies and on TV? When I was a kid, which was pre-TV, I'd go to the Saturday-afternoon movies and watch the sports news to see sixty seconds of college football highlights. At times, I'd stay through two double features just to see the sports news again, and Glenn Davis, the All-American halfback at Army, weave explosively through the line into the open field and score another beautifully executed touchdown. Then I'd go home and pretend I was Glenn Davis. Today it's all there for kids to see on TV with replays, slow motion, commentary, and an overall wealth of information. Today, movie and sports stars still influence young people, who often copy their habits, traits, and language. Do the same with your heroes and role models in business and life.

I don't mean be a clone, but if you admire the way your boss or some other executive makes a presentation, runs a meeting, or deals with other people, why not copy those strengths? This is an excellent way to learn.

In addition to those who can in some way shape your career, role models can also be the leading business leaders and strategists. In addition to TV documentaries, there are many good movies, books, and more that portray the best in business. Any of them can become your role models.

Even beyond the obvious leaders such as Bill Gates of Microsoft,

Carly Fiorina, CEO of Hewlett-Packard, and Eddie Lampert, CEO of ESL, the company that merged Sears and Kmart, there are role models at middle management levels offering more practical lessons. Several organizations, such as the nonprofit American Management Association (www.amanet.org) and many universities, have video and DVD programs where you can watch the experts in action.

Role models also can be historical figures. I recently met a young man who talked in depth about Thomas Jefferson, and I also know a successful woman who could tell me anything about Thomas Edison.

Recently, three of the most successful athletes finished their spectacular careers: Cal Ripken, Tony Gwynn, and Mia Hamm. The same characteristics they displayed in sports apply to business and in life. Watching them handle their fame and record-setting careers in such a humble and honest way is a learning exercise for all of us.

There are ample opportunities to find a role model, though, in your job—anyone at any level who does impressive things you may want to emulate. These connections will enrich your work environment and life.

You can also see examples of job performance and behavior that you don't want to copy. These anti-role models are valuable examples of what not to do. You must distinguish them and recognize these anti-role models when you see them. They are cancers that will destroy everyone around them and can go undetected for quite some time. Once these anti-role models are discovered, you must act because the damage will be great if no action is taken. These type of people are hard to describe because each comes with a different set of problems and clues. What is common, though, is the dissension and low morale that results from their actions. They spread dangerous rumors to destroy or damage someone who is perceived as a threat and also tell lies intended to enhance themselves.

The anti-role models must be detected and terminated. Transfers or watching and waiting are not good options. I've known only a few in my career, and in those cases actions were taken too late and much damage was done.

While not as dangerous as the anti-role model, there are people who are difficult to work with or who are overly political. In my experience as a manager, they sometimes can be rehabilitated, but the odds are probably against it. Personalities don't change. If they have unusually valuable skills or knowledge, than you may want to make the effort. However, you may find it more effective to find better people to do their work.

Throughout your career, role models can help you improve. Always be open and receptive to learning from those who excel at their jobs.

You are or could be a role model at some point in your career. Think of the implications. The skills and habits you learn from this book will make you a good role model. Don't miss the opportunity!

REMEMBER THIS

Role models are all around you or available to you through TV, video and DVD training courses, newspapers, magazines, etc. Recognize and emulate them, but be selective and use multiple opportunities to learn and adopt positive traits and skills.

"Example is not the main thing for influencing others.
It is the only thing."
— Albert Schweitzer

"It is well to respect the leader. Learn from him. Observe him.
Study him. But don't worship him. Believe you can surpass.
Believe you can go beyond. Those who harbor the second-best attitude
are invariably second-best doers."
— David J. Schwartz

"People seldom improve when they have no other model
but themselves to copy after."
—Oliver Goldsmith

26. REVIEW YOUR CAREER

Recall People Who Have Helped You Along the Way

I can remember very clearly all the people who made a difference for me. Several years ago I sketched a chart that traced my job history by dates, companies, positions held, and income. I also wrote in names of the people along the way that I'll always remember for their significant help. I recommend you do this valuable exercise for yourself. They may be a role model for you to follow in helping others. These people can probably be categorized in terms of what kind of help they provided and what skills and habits you admire. Knowing all this can help you to be more like them.

I see the people on my list as teachers, sponsors, or role models. Caring and sincere, many had a desire to reach out and help. Often genuine friendships were developed.

Each person on my list had particular skills and traits that I admired. Some were influential role models achieving high levels of success and displaying many notable qualities. Their personalities were each different, and they were, for the most part, ambitious. Some were willing teachers and genuinely supportive and generous with their time. They didn't all move to the top, but they played key roles in my career and for their companies. They fostered teamwork and high morale in everyone they worked with, especially the newer employees. You need people like them—unselfish coaches and contributors—in your organization. Although they were not all individually role models, I learned from them just the same.

I recommend you take the time to do this instructive exercise. Companies can't survive and compete without these solid performers holding it together and providing a common thread of support. There is real value in writing down what you learned and see again the people who influenced you and how they did. **Wouldn't you like to be on someone's good list?**

REMEMBER THIS

Recording the history of those who influenced and helped you clearly brings back many good memories— and can help you be a better person.

"I don't know what your destiny will be, but one thing I do know: The only ones among you who will really be happy are those who have sought and found how to serve."
— Albert Schweitzer

"We can do anything we want if we stick to it long enough."
— Helen Keller

"For every one of us that succeeds, it's because there's somebody there to show you the way out. The light doesn't always necessarily have to be in your family; for me it was teachers and school."
— Oprah Winfrey

TIME	COMPANY	MY JOBS	WHO HELPED AND INFLUENCED/ ROLE MODELS
1949–1953	Rutgers University	Student	**Walt Leib**-High school star athlete and buddy two years ahead of me, who shepherded me through freshman year. Helped increase my scholarship, got me a job, and always had positive attitude.
1953–1956	U.S. Air Force	1st Lt. Intelligence Group of 17th Airforce	**Lt./Col. Boris Zubko**-Taught me how to write concise and factual reports.
1956–1964	N.J. Bell Tel. Co.	Traffic Engineer & Systems Analyst	**Len Bishop**-division management. I learned how effective his ease of communicating was to any level. His sincerity came through.
			Bill Clancey-regional manager. I learned perseverance and attention to detail.
			Charlie Hugel-regional manager. He later became highly successful CEO of a few companies yet he never lost contact with his peers. Friendly, commanding, and sense of humor.
			Ted Simis-division manager. Provided great support and always knew latest management tools. A student and friend of Peter Drucker.
			Charlie Schlenger-Personal, caring support from a veteran.
			Gene Thomson-supervisor. Tough, caring interest in my career. Good teacher.
			Sterling Kerr-supervisor. Taught me about creativity in presentations and how to enthusiastically sell your programs.
1960–1961 (Recalled to Active Duty)	U.S. Air Force	Major, Director of Intelligence for 108th Fighter Bomber Wing	**Col. James Salter**-Taught me about organization, planning, and discipline. A role model for an executive in the military. He later became a highly successful novelist.
			Major General Donald Strait-Role model for leadership and management skills. Later became president of Republic Aviation.
1964–1981	ITT	Puerto Rico Tel. Co. Asst. Controller; World Communications, Data Transmission Systems, Dir. of Operations, Dir. of Engineering; V.P. Data Services Latin America	**Harold Geneen**-CEO and chairman. I learned how one person could totally dominate and lead a large corporation of over $20 billion. Famed for his attention to detail and facts. I learned to set high standards for myself and others.

128

TIME	COMPANY	MY JOBS	WHO HELPED AND INFLUENCED/ ROL
1964–1981	ITT	Corporate consulting; Aetna Consumer Finance, Dir. of Planning	**Herb Kolber**-Was loyal, had gr gave me every benefit of his knc role model and strong leader. Ch took charge. **Fred Gibbs**-executive vice presic tent, great presence as leader. **George Knapp**-president. Puerto learned how wit and humor play b top down.
1981–1989	Burger King Corp.	Executive V.P. and Chief Adm. Officer	**Jeff Campbell**-CEO. Taught me th planning and presentation skills. **Herb Kolber**-president internationa closest personal support one could as **Norman Brinker**-Pillsbury board m founder of "Steak & Ale" and "Bennig successful restaurant entrepreneur, whd many new restaurant concepts such as believer in self-development, use of ou seminars, and constant learning and trai and teach his employees. **Charlie Olcott**-president. I learned mor skills and the value of positive attitude, e personal courage. **Jerry Ruenheck**-president. As president time to compliment my efforts. Down to one respected and liked his leadership styl **Ron McDougall**-Now chairman of Brinl International. He had it all and was always l and supportive.
1989–1992	Burger King	Consultant	**Nigel Travis**-senior vice president of humai resources. I learned how the British look at c structure and their value system versus the Ar one. Different cultures and different strategies. **Barry Gibbons**-CEO. Was the new chairman me how a free spirit could influence a major c tion in some good ways.
1992–2003	Seegott, Inc.	Senior V.P. Marketing and Planning	**Paul Seegott**-CEO and founder. I learned from highly successful entrepreneur about dealing wit people and the value of establishing relationships having big goals. Vision and creativity from the tc

129

27. STRIVE TO BE FAIR

Win-Win Feels Good for Everyone

It helps to have a simple measurement to guide our behavior for business and also life. The one that works for me is the rule of fairness. When you are deciding on an issue, the question should be, "Is it really fair?"

For example, you recently got a pay raise and are not satisfied. You must objectively decide if it is fair. If you decide it isn't, you have a few options. You can discuss it professionally with your boss, or you can live with it and try to do better. I believe the answer is to talk to your boss in a non-aggressive, professional tone.

For our discussion of fairness as a good management guideline, I include examples of unfairness to show the impact of decisions. The reality is that there are many fair decisions, including the following that I'll always remember.

When I was with New Jersey Bell Telephone Company early in my career, I received an annual salary adjustment at the end of my second year. The following month I was promoted and received another increase. I was obviously appreciative but couldn't believe that I received two increases in the period of one month. My supervisor assured me that my good fortune was only fair because they were two separate rewards.

The fairness rule plays an important role in negotiations, such as an acquisition your company is making. You expect to be treated fairly and

given complete, correct information in order to make the right decisions. Unfortunately, this often doesn't happen. Sometimes details may be withheld or disguised. This isn't fair, but it happens. Comprehensive due diligence should produce what you need to know. When you find that the rule of fairness isn't being followed, be prepared for some unpleasant surprises.

Many issues and events will be subject to the fairness rule, but you must remember that many decisions and results may not be fair. Sometimes, you've had no role to play and yet must live with the consequence. If you find that the decision seriously violated the rule of fairness, you may be able to present an argument that overturns it. Rules or decisions that hurt people can also harm the company, so don't take everything at face value. You might have to step forward and raise some questions. I've seen a couple of cases where compensation plans that turned out to be unfair were changed when the evidence was presented.

The guideline of fairness becomes even more important, though, when you are in the position to make a decision or implement a program. During the process, you might ask, "Is it fair to everyone? Is it a win-win situation?"

We all know that events in life and business are not always fair. One situation in particular brought this home to me. ITT was transferring me from Denver, Colorado, to New York City. I was eager to take this job but concerned about the much higher cost of living, especially in housing. I spoke to those responsible for making cost-of-living adjustments about how important it was to maintain a similar lifestyle for my family. In spite of my effort, when they made the adjustment, it was short by a few thousand dollars. This shortfall limited the mortgage we could carry. In short, the decision was not fair and took the wind out of my sails.

When the rule of fairness is not applied, the loss of enthusiasm, productivity, and a positive attitude can be difficult to measure financially.

Unfairness can damage a company. I am thinking of companies that use the law to allow them to treat their employees unfairly, especially young employees who should be encouraged and trained, which would result in lower turnover and higher revenues. Instead they are treated as expendables, given little training, few career options, and a compensation plan that doesn't reward productivity. If the company treated their employees as valuable assets, the company would benefit from a loyal, competent, and stable base. The smart companies invest in their people, treat them fairly, and reap the financial rewards for it.

When you have been rewarded or treated fairly, you remember those times clearly and you know what a difference it made in your attitude and performance.

The measure of fairness is not always in your control. You learn from experience, and this can help you when you have the authority to make decisions. In those cases where you are not in control, you win some, and you lose some. At times, you can discuss or appeal your case and may win.

REMEMBER THIS

Using the question, "Is it fair?" can guide you every day. This measure implies many things. When you can say it is fair, you stand on safe and solid ground.

"To make no mistakes is not in the power of man; but from their errors and mistakes the wise and good learn wisdom for the future."

— Plutarch

"It's discouraging to think how many people are shocked by honesty and how few by deceit."

— Noel Coward

"Try not to become a man of success but rather try to become a man of value."

— Albert Einstein

28. DEVELOP FAITH FOR THE TOUGH TIMES

Everybody Has Them

Y ou will find much in your work rewarding and enjoyable, but there are also times of stress and disappointment. In those times, you need an inner strength and confidence to keep you going. **You need to be prepared for the tough times just as you prepare for bad weather.**

I knew a CEO of a major company who was placed in a difficult position when his company was the target of an unfriendly acquisition. To avoid the takeover, a leveraged buy-out was attempted, requiring major capital from an investment bank. In order to secure this funding, the CEO was asked to testify to a financial forecast that predicted very ambitious results over the next three years. He knew the numbers were not achievable, but also realized he would not get the funding without his convincing testimony. The CEO had two options: lie about the numbers and probably get the funding, or tell the truth and lose the funding.

In the first case, his misleading statements would have been lies, and he and his top staff people would have known it. This course would have likely secured the funding. In the second option, his non-support of the financial forecast would kill the buy-out and also guarantee his termination from the company.

The man refused to lie and lost his job. He could have taken the easy way out, guaranteeing a softer landing with golden parachute and enough to secure his financial future. His value system wouldn't let him do this, and he paid the consequences.

He chose the second option, based on his character, faith, and what he considered to be right and wrong. These values continue to carry him forward, and although he suffered financial setbacks, his wife and children also support his value system and share his strong faith.

When I worked for ITT in Rio de Janeiro, Brazil, in the early 1970s, I was fortunate to meet Billy Graham and three of his key associates, George Beverly Shea, the singer; Cliff Barrows, the announcer and director of music; and Henry Holly, the Crusade director. They were there for Billy Graham's 1974 Crusade in Rio de Janeiro. My close friend Wally Williams was pastor of the local English-language church; he asked us if we could host a dinner for the group. What I learned from those three men was the depth of their commitment, and the detailed **preparation and planning** that had taken place over a one-year period for Graham's five-day crusade. I have rarely seen people with these men's **skills in communicating** at all levels and the **ability to really listen** with full attention. They were **reliable, positive,** and fully understood that **work was not an eight-hour day.** True **role models,** they spent a lot of time **learning** about everything. They clearly had a **measure to live by** and were supported by their **faith.**

There are many stories of people who have survived and even prospered due to a strong faith. Faith is likely to be associated with a formal religion, and I don't pretend to understand many of them. I only know that faith gives you the strength to deal with the low points in business and in life.

I recommend that you read the classic *The Power of Positive Thinking* (Ballantine Books), written many years ago by the late Dr. Norman Vincent Peale. One of the first self-development books, this practical, direct-action manual teaches techniques on dealing with people and adversity in a practical, meaningful way.

REMEMBER THIS

Having a faith that works for you will give you the strength to survive the low points in business and in your life. The source of that faith is up to you.

"Without faith, nothing is possible. With it, nothing is impossible."
— Mary McLeod Bethune

"Physical strength can never permanently withstand the impact of spiritual force."
— Franklin D. Roosevelt

"When it is dark enough, you can see the stars."
— Charles Beard

RECAP

Profile of a Successful Person

Being successful demands a lot of effort and time. Talent certainly helps, but this alone is often not enough. In the previous pages, I've described a few talented executives who fell short of their potential because they lacked commonsense work habits and tools. I've also outlined many fundamental skills and traits to help you greatly enhance your performance and career and become a more well-rounded person. If you use the information in this book, the descriptions below are how you will be described by your managers and associates. It's a glowing picture of a fast-track employee.

- You are known as a **diligent problem-solver** who can **present the unshakable facts.** You are considered a valuable asset to your company.

- You **recognize change,** possibly before others, and deal with it to help your company and yourself.

- You are **better prepared for your meetings** and are a key contributor because of your groundwork and knowledge.

- You are known for your **positive and agreeable attitude,** and people want to work with you.

- You realize that rewards don't come automatically and there are times to **ask for what you deserve.**

- You understand the importance of being **able to communicate**

effectively to sell yourself and your ideas.

- You are considered **reliable and responsive.** Being dependable has enhanced your reputation.

- You are known as a considerate person who **cares for others.** People respond favorably to you.

- You know how to **respond in both victory and defeat.** People admire you for your behavior in both.

- You recognize the **importance of presenting your work** and yourself in the best way. You maximize your opportunities and reputation.

- You know what is important about **your business and its vital life signs.** As a result, your work is more focused and valuable, enhancing your image.

- You take the time to **plan and think about your career.** You approach your work with a long-term view. You try to avoid leaving important career issues to pure chance.

- You are a team player and recognize that **you can't do it alone.** You know that you must enlist the help of others. People see you as cooperative and productive.

- **You enjoy your work** because you have learned some things to make your job more interesting and fun.

- You are **curious about the world around you,** follow the national and international news, and find that this new knowledge opens up doors professionally and socially.

- **You are open and friendly** and recognize that honey is better than vinegar when you approach people and problems. You know patience pays dividends compared to anger and confrontation.

- You have learned that promises met are powerful for your career and image—and that **actions speak louder than words.** Many around you don't meet these standards.

- **You have helped others to succeed** and are known as a team player. You have a good relationship with your boss, and your support is appreciated.

- **You realize you can learn from others** and have become much more observant, identifying **good role models** for yourself.

- You are known as **a person who goes beyond the eight-hour day** and that your commitment is greater than your associates'. You know that success is the result of more effort than others are willing to make.

- You are **someone who always wants to learn.** This has set you apart from your associates and helps to strengthen your reputation.

- **People describe you as being fair** in all your dealings, and your value system is becoming known.

When reviewing this long list of favorable descriptions, would there be any surprise that you are viewed as one with strong fundamental strengths, values, and skills who is a real asset to your company?

This is a powerful endorsement of you and your abilities and even being identified with half of these statements would give you a profile that few of your associates possess.

Looking at that long list you also realize that you probably enjoy your work far more and feel your increased value will help you build a successful career. You feel good about yourself.

Now you see how success can be simplified. Good luck and the best to you.

REMEMBER THIS

Being recognized for having successful habits, traits, disciplines, and skills can serve as a strong endorsement and build your reputation. They can also make your job more manageable and enjoyable—and not having them can jeopardize your career.

"Keep away from people who try to belittle your ambitions. Small people always do that, but the really great make you feel that you, too, can become great."
— Mark Twain

"What you get by achieving your goals is not as important as what you become by achieving your goals."
— Zig Ziglar

"Keep your thoughts positive,
because your thoughts become your words.
Keep your words positive,
because your words become your behaviors.
Keep your behaviors positive,
because your behaviors become your habits.
Keep your habits positive,
because your habits become your values.
Keep your values positive,
because your values become your destiny."
— Mahatma Gandhi

SUMMARY

Part One—Professional Practices to Get You Noticed

1. Present the Unshakable Facts
Correct decisions depend upon them.

You cannot make the correct decision without hard facts. Too often people believe they have the facts when they don't, and the results can be damaging to the company and individuals.

2. Use Information to Reach Good Conclusions
Gather it, analyze it, and make a plan to take action.

The military intelligence cycle is a logical way to gather and examine information, search for facts, and reach conclusions that can be productively used to make decisions.

3. Tackle Problems Head-On
Simplify by looking at them in pieces.

Problem-solving can be complex but can be simplified if you can look at it in pieces. Whether you use flow charts, diagrams, or ask questions that dig deeper for more facts, keep your efforts organized and logical.

4. Communicate Confidently
In speech and writing, be clear and interesting.

You must communicate to succeed. Speaking and writing skills are essential. Learn what you do right and what you do wrong, then, if necessary, get some help. Do whatever you can to be the best communicator.

5. Don't Try to Go It Alone
Support and cooperation will get the job done.

The support and cooperation from the people around you will greatly determine your success. Don't try to go it alone. Use the best talent to brainstorm and help on projects. Delegate and recognize all contributions. Extend your network beyond your normal boundaries.

6. Track Vital Life Signs
Learn what makes a company in your industry financially sound.

The vital life signs of your company and industry are essential for you to know. This knowledge will help you to be more effective and to be recognized as someone who is on the ball.

7. Be an Eager Learner
The more you know, the more valuable you are.

Learn from everything. Your quest to know more should never stop. Know what's important in the local, national, and world news. You will perform your job better and brighten your life.

8. Ask for What you Want
Don't expect rewards to come automatically.

If what you request is fair and practical, there is nothing wrong with asking for it. It happens all the time in sales when you ask for an order or when you pitch your services to a client. In any case, asking will improve your chances—and not asking could mean it won't happen.

9. Package Yourself for Sale
Present yourself and your work in the best light possible.

You must sell yourself and your work. Packaging it all successfully is how you do it. Perception is reality, so take your best step forward. It is no small effort, but you must take the time to do it right.

10. Plan Your Career *Keep your skills marketable.*	It is up to you to plan your career and the steps needed to be successful. The earlier the better, but a late start is better than no start. Be valuable and marketable wherever you are and keep your horizons broad. Your networks are important but not a substitute for having goals.
11. Prepare for Meetings *This is the most important thing that can set you apart.*	You must be well prepared before a meeting or planning session. This takes prior effort and hard work. If this doesn't happen, the meeting is unlikely to produce good results. The "pre" part before any meeting or planning can make or break it.
12. Get Involved in Company Planning *There is no substitute for good planning.*	Planning is essential and needs to be more than just an exercise. Success requires constant monitoring and adjustments. If circumstances cause a plan to change dramatically, so be it. Don't follow plans blindly if they don't make sense anymore. Get involved in the process and learn what and how your company is planning.
13. Network with Consultants *Be sure the goal is clear.*	Consultants can be very useful if they resolve a clearly stated need and can obtain the hands-on information from the operations staff. In addition, they make useful contacts for your network because of their knowledge and broad-range of contacts.
14. Sharpen Your Management Skills *Learn how to minimize people problems.*	Managing is a great opportunity where you will learn, help others, and be helped. A good value system and common sense will serve you well. Watch, ask questions and rely on those above you and below you; managing is a skill best learned on the job.

Part Two—Personal Traits and Practices to Develop

15. Have a Positive Attitude *The personal trait that dominates.*	Never underestimate the power of a positive attitude. Learn to be comfortable in social situations, to be sincere, to be optimistic, and to be polite. Combine this with good work and you increase the probability of success.
16. Be Responsive and Reliable *Two of the most basic essentials.*	There is no substitute for being responsive. It builds on your reputation for being reliable and can only help your career. Being reliable and responsive are two of the very basic traits you should be known for. They require discipline and attention to organization. The consequences of not having them will limit your career.
17. Be a Doer, Not Just a Talker *Step forward and volunteer.*	Step forward, volunteer, commit, and then do it. Many people talk and promise, but few actually deliver. If you do, you will stand out from the crowd.
18. Anticipate and Adapt to Change *Transform yourself.*	Change is a fact of work life. You should not ignore change but deal with it everyday. Watch for change, recognize it and its effect on your job, and develop plans for how to deal with it in your company and your career.
19. Be Open and Friendly *Honey gets better results than vinegar.*	You are looking for results in one way or another. You are always more likely to get them using honey—open, friendly behavior—than vinegar—anger and fear. The results you get from vinegar may produce some immediate success, but the long-lasting effects will produce a lingering bad taste with many people you're going to need along the way.

20. Put in Extra Time and Effort
The road to success is open 24/7.

Achieving success takes more time than a 9-to-5 day allows. You must sacrifice some of your free time and put in the extra effort, but if you love your job, you won't consider it a sacrifice.

21. Help People
Including your boss.

Help others just as people help you. You can't lose and have much to gain. You learn when you help and the one supported will remember. Helping your boss has multiple benefits and could increase your success along with the boss's. If you don't help an associate or your boss, expect negative consequences.

22. Have a Caring Heart
What comes around goes around.

In the course of doing business, you will work with many people. You help them, and they help and support you. Doing this on an impersonal basis is a disadvantage to both of you. A close, caring bond is not only more productive, but the teamwork and a family environment created help all the players.

23. Be Gracious at Winning and Losing
No one likes a bragger or a whiner.

Be prepared for both victories and defeats. Handle each with dignity and continue to be gracious to all your associates. Show yourself to be a winner, no matter what the circumstances are.

24. Learn to Enjoy Your Work
If you can't, look elsewhere; don't retire on the job.

If you don't enjoy your work and your job, it is unlikely that you will succeed. You must take the initiative to make it better. Communication and a positive attitude are the two tools to make it happen

25. Choose the Best Role Models
Learn from people who know more than you do.

Role models are all around you or available to you through TV, video and DVD training courses, newspapers, magazines, etc. Recognize and emulate them, but be selective and use multiple opportunities to learn and adopt positive traits and skills.

26. Review Your Career
Recall people who have helped you along the way.

Recording the history of those who influenced and helped you clearly brings back many good memories—and can help you be a better person.

27. Strive to Be Fair
Win-win feels good for everyone.

Using the question, "Is it fair?" can guide you every day. This measure implies many things. When you can say it is fair, you stand on safe and solid ground.

28. Develop Faith for the Tough Times
Everybody has them.

Having a faith that works for you will give you the strength to survive the low points in business and in your life. The source of that faith is up to you.

Recap
Profile of a Successful Person.

Being recognized for having successful habits, traits, disciplines and skills can serve as a strong endorsement and build your reputation. They also can make your job more manageable and enjoyable—and not having them can jeopardize your career.